Fran

From an abused childhood
to the abundant life

A Story of God's Victory

By Fran Lance
with Pat King

Women's Aglow Fellowship
Lynnwood, WA 98036

Cover Photo by Tom Palidar

Foreword

I 've known Fran Lance from the time we met that special day in Nancy Rogers' living room with about fifty other women present. Since then both of us have had extremely busy lives but we've managed to keep in touch at least a couple of times a year, at birthdays and Christmas time, anyway.

Reading of Fran's early years was a revelation. I knew she had had a difficult childhood, but I didn't realize just *how* difficult. I saw how God took the ingredients of confusion, fear, loneliness, hate, rebellion, emptiness, promiscuity, poverty, abandonment, despair and turned them into clarity, love, satisfaction, obedience, fulfillment, self-control, prosperity, trust, joy. He turned the water of her life into wine. God's age-old miracle is still working.

Many people are afraid to come to God because they view Him as a moral policeman . . . one who's out to take their fun away. Because of my faulty understanding I, too, saw God|that|way|during|my teen-age years and early twenties. But then I found even though you've strayed a million miles away, or it seems that far, it's only one step back into His waiting arms.

Some may say Fran has written a very "gutsy" book, but often life is that way. In her book there's nothing pompous, no skirting around the facts. She tells it like it was and is. If you don't like reality, conflict, miracles, and excitement you won't like this book.

I think you'll like it. I know I did. I hope Fran's book will be for many of you that one step into God's arms of love and total acceptance.

Rita Bennett

1

Preface

God can make something of your life.
You are special to Him.

While your mother was wondering if you would be a boy or a girl, wondering if you would have blue eyes or brown, wondering if you would have ten fingers and ten toes, God knew you and loved you, and you were special to Him.

Before you were born, God saw your life spread out before Him. He knew all about the lust, the greed and the pride that would trap you. He knew the unfair situations of your childhood, or your teen years, or your adult life. He knew you would suffer pain that no person should ever have to suffer at the hands of another. He saw the loneliness, the fear, the rejection.

Even knowing what was ahead for you He knit you together within your mother.[1] You were specially made as no other person has been made before or since. God was present at your birth, and He has never left you all these long years. Through your pain, His sorrow was greater than your own.

However, He had an advantage you didn't have. He knew the future. He could see the healing that would make you "weller than well." He could see the beautiful woman you would become. He could see how He was going to take all your pain and make something beautiful out of it.

His plan for your life would be worked out through the sometimes strange circumstances of your family, your friends, your schooling, your marriage, your children, your finances or the lack of any of these things. Even though He didn't want you to suffer He knew He would take that suffering and use if for your own good. In God's plan and from His viewpoint nothing is wasted. No matter what has happened in your life God is able to use it all for your own good and for His glory.

You may say, "Not me, if only you knew what I've been through, if only you knew how I've been hurt, if only you knew what awful things I've done, you'd know that God couldn't possibly make anything out of my life." You may say, "If you knew me you'd know that I couldn't possibly be special enough for Him to make me into something beautiful."

But He can. He wants to and He is able to do it. I know this for sure. He took the ugly mess of my life and did a miracle. There was hardly any hope for me the way things were . . . but, let me tell you my story . . .

Chapter 1

"Mama, wake up. It's me, Fran. I'm hungry . . . can you wake up now?"

Mama moaned and turned over but her eyes didn't open. It was after noon and I hadn't eaten anything yet. My older sister, Linda, who was eight, and my brother, Fred, who was six had gone off to school leaving me and little Dottie alone. Mama had come home during the night drunk and I still couldn't budge her.

I looked across the hall where two-year-old Dottie was curled up on the bed the four of us shared, sleeping at last. She had cried all morning until I'd found a piece of bread in the kitchen and given it to her. Gobbling it down, she'd whimpered herself to sleep.

I sat there beside Mama, pushing her dark hair from her lined face. I placed my hand gently on her cheek and looked around the room. There was the high dresser where my father had kept Hershey bars and marshmallows in the top drawer when he'd been alive. There was the vanity in the corner with its mottled, broken mirror. By turning just a little I could see myself in it. I wished I was pretty like my mother. Instead, I was too skinny; everyone said so. But I did peer carefully at my eyes because that was the one good thing about me. Everyone said they were pretty and blue.

I picked up a comb with half the teeth missing. It was like some of the old, toothless men who came to my mother's bedroom at night. I tried to comb my blonde hair but the snarls just broke off more teeth. I thought that maybe when Linda came home she'd comb my hair for me so it wouldn't be so matted and messed up.

Under my blue cotton dress I could hear my stomach rumbling so loudly I decided to fix my own breakfast. I was sure Mama would be proud of me when she woke up and found what I could do all by myself. In the icebox I found an egg. Next, I found a pan and put some water in it. Pushing a chair to the stove I climbed on it so I could reach the knob. I put the pan on the burner and got down and got the egg, climbed up on the chair again and put the egg in the water.

I wasn't sure how long to wait. I got down and went to look at Mama and Dottie again. Then I tried combing my hair. I was feeling so hungry I couldn't wait any longer. With a great feeling of achievement I took the egg out of the pan with a spoon and put it in a dish. Then carrying it carefully I took it to the table and cracked it open with a knife. The egg oozed all over the dish and the shell. I ate it quickly. Then I licked the shell, the dish and my fingers. I felt warm and not so hungry any more and I was proud of being four years old and able to cook.

Just as I was licking the last speck of yellow yolk off the table, Mama appeared in the doorway and staggered to the chair. "Mama, look what I did." I jumped up and down in anticipation of approval. "I fixed an egg by myself." Then I stood real quiet so I wouldn't miss what she said.

She looked at me and tears slid down her cheeks. She sobbed, "Oh, my poor baby."

Terrible disappointment flooded me as I stood there in bewilderment. I'd wanted her to appreciate me and hug me and tell me I was wonderful. Instead I'd only done something to make her cry.

Looking back it seems most of my childhood memories were laced with either disappointment or fear. I remember waking up one morning and finding that Mama was not in her bed. She wasn't on the sofa or the floor either.

"Where's Mama?" I asked Linda.

"She didn't come home last night."

"Where is she?"

"I don't know," Linda sighed, "and I don't even care."

Both she and Fred stayed home from school that day to take care of Dottie and me. Mama didn't come home that night either. The next morning I woke up before Linda and Fred. I crawled out of our communal bed and went to look at Mama's bed. It was still empty.

I woke up Linda, "She's not home yet," I whispered.

Linda groaned, "Oh, Fran, I hope the neighbors haven't noticed."

I knew what she meant. If the neighbors guessed we were alone for very long, they'd call the police and then we'd all be in trouble. All three of us big kids knew that the police were our enemies. Mama was scared to death of them, and we knew from her that they caused nothing but trouble.

The day was only half over when Linda's fears were realized. Fred came running into the kitchen where Linda was emptying the last of the canned milk into Dottie's bottle. "It's the police," he warned us in a whisper. "They stopped in front." Without a word Linda grabbed Dottie, and Fred grabbed me. The four of us fled to the closet in the hall.

As we crouched in a huddle on the floor, Dottie started whimpering. "Shsh," Linda commanded and clamped her hand over Dottie's mouth.

The police knocked on the door and then began to bang. My heart pounded against my chest. What if they found us? What awful thing would happen? In a few minutes we heard their footsteps coming onto the back porch and we could hear their deep voices. I imagined them staring in the windows. I kept holding my breath, too frightened to cry. It seemed like an unbearable length of time until the voices and pounding ceased.

At last Linda opened the closet door and pried her hand off of Dottie's mouth. Dottie went limp in her arms. Linda, in her own fright, hadn't realized that her tightly clasped hand had cut off Dottie's oxygen. Linda laid Dottie on the floor, and I stood looking at her. She was such a pathetic thing, lying there with her head back, all blue and lifeless. Forgotten were the police and the scary darkness of the closet. My heart pounded with a new fear. What if Dottie was dead?

Linda got down on her knees and shook her, "Dottie, wake up," she cried, "Oh, Dottie, wake up."

I could hardly breathe myself until at last, Dottie opened her eyes. She reached her arms up to Linda who sat on the floor and gathered us all into her lap.

The next morning when I woke up Mama was home in her bed.

I don't believe Mama ever intended to get trapped into prostitution. She had been the cream-of-the-crop in her own family of six children, the pretty one, the one who was smart in school. Even though the family was poor, split by divorce and the children were in and out of foster homes, everyone expected Mama to have a good life.

She'd met my father in a logging camp and despite the predictions theirs was a stormy marriage from the first. Linda could remember times when Mama set the table, prepared dinner and arranged her hair prettily only to have Dad not show up for hours. She could remember how Mama made glittering Christmas decorations out of old scraps of tin and sold them to buy groceries during the times my father didn't come at all.

She remembered, too, when Mama took in washing to pay the bills during those depression days after my father was killed. Then Mama told Linda that the welfare said she had to turn over the money she made to them. That was so discouraging Mama quit doing the extra wash.

After that the men started coming to our house, sporadically at first, and then more often. Mama's drinking became correspondingly worse.

Because Mama wanted to protect us from her lifestyle she had a rule that was not to be broken. When a man was in her bedroom with her, us kids were not to disturb her for any reason at all.

One time I was playing in her room and had crawled under her bed to get a toy. Just then I heard Mama and a man come in and close the door behind them. I stayed where I was, keeping as quiet as could be. As I crouched there in the semi-darkness, afraid of being discovered, feeling tense and trapped, a loud clatter seemed to shake the room. There, on the floor, half under the bed beside me, had dropped a splintery, brown, wooden leg. I lay staring at it in utter horror, not daring to touch it.

Between the sounds from the bed that I couldn't understand and this horrible wooden appendage, I was even more terrified than I'd been that day hiding in the closet. In fear, I waited until all was quiet and I could sneak past the wooden monster, out of her room and back into the safety of my sisters and brother.

Mama had no way of knowing the jeopardy her activities placed us in. The landlord's son, a fuzzy-whiskered boy of sixteen, caused the greatest fear of all in my young life.

He seemed to know when a man was with Mama and we children had no protection. I can remember how he'd come and sit beside the bed after the others were asleep. His hands touched all over my body while I lay there stiff with shame. I knew what was happening was wrong, but I was afraid to call out. He pinned me down while I endured the frightening feeling of his whiskers between my legs. When he was gone, I wanted to get my mother and put my arms around her and cry and cry. But I knew that I was never, ever to disturb her when a man was in her room.

Despite all that went on in our lives I felt certain my mother loved me as much as I loved her. Sometimes she would hold me on her lap and pat my head over and over. Those were precious moments, the bits and pieces

I remembered in the hard times ahead.

The idea of suicide obsessed her. When I was four she tried to end her life by jumping off a bridge. She plunged into the water and landed close to a fisherman's boat. He fished her out of the water, unconscious but alive. She was forced to go on.

One day when Linda and Fred were at school she sent me into the bathroom for a razor. She cried aloud, saying that life was rotten and that she was a failure. I put the razor on the table beside her wine bottle.

Without hesitating she picked it up and slashed at her wrist. I don't remember seeing any blood but I still remember myself trembling all over. I had no idea what to do. Mama looked at my forlorn face and tried to explain. "Oh, Fran, I have to do it, I can't go on." Once again her suicide attempt didn't succeed, and once again she had to face responsibility that must have seemed more than she could possibly bear.

Again, Mama tried to kill herself. Only this time the consequences were far more reaching. While we children played outside, she turned on all the gas jets on the stove. Then she went to bed, hoping never to wake up again.

I don't know how she was discovered but the next thing I knew, a red fire engine zoomed to our house and squealed to a stop. Firemen raced past us kids and up the stairs. Two police cars followed, their sirens blaring. The neighbors streamed out of their houses and into our yard. I knew inside of me that something had happened to Mama, but I was too afraid to move from the sandbox where I was playing. Out of the corner of my eye I saw the firemen carry a stretcher through the doorway and lay it on the porch. I knew Mama was on it. The fireman gave her oxygen, and I went right on playing.

I remember the whispers of the neighbors. "Suicide," they said, "she tried it again." I held my breath. Then with relief I heard someone else say, "Well, she didn't succeed. Too bad."

The next thing I knew the four of us were huddled in the back of one of the police cars. "I hope she did kill herself this time," Linda announced, "I hope I never see her again." I could understand what Linda was saying, but I couldn't agree. No matter what Mama had done, I loved her and I wanted to be able to see her again someday. But for Linda the responsibility was too much for one little eight-year-old girl. So far, for all of us, life was almost too hard to bear. Yet, when we were taken from Mama, the pain to come would even be harder to endure.

[1]Psalm 139:13-14

Chapter 2

The further the police car took us the more excited I became. Mother would be okay—the firemen were taking care of her. The policemen were friendly which was an unexpected surprise. Most comforting of all was snuggling next to Linda and Fred and holding Dottie's little pink hand in my own. I settled down deciding to enjoy the day's adventure.

Almost before I knew it we had stopped in front of a large grey building. Inside, Fred was taken away immediately into a section for boys. Just before the door closed between us he looked back at Linda and me with a scared look all over his face. Fear closed its fingers around me. I knew that six years old was pretty big so if Fred was scared then so was I. I grabbed Linda's hand and held it tightly.

"Such skinny little things you girls are," the matron of the Children's Home announced as we peeled off our undershirts. She took our clothes and stuffed them in a laundry bag, then handed us the Home's clothes to wear. I pulled on unfamiliar rough underwear and slid a faded navy blue dress over my head. I felt strange in these other clothes, not at all like myself.

When we girls were changed we were taken to our beds. There in the biggest room I'd ever seen were two endless rows of beds, all exactly alike, all of them way up high off the floor. It was several days before I could remember which one was mine and even longer till I could climb in and out without being afraid of falling. I felt lonely and lost there, without my clothes, without Fred, without the comfort of all of us cozy as four peas in a pod in bed at night.

What I hated most about the Home was waking up in the morning. When I was with my mother it never mattered if I woke up wet or not. She didn't care and neither did Linda nor Fred. Now it mattered a whole lot.

The housemother didn't want anyone to be wet. My first conscious thought each morning was, "Did I wet the bed?" I'd wiggle a little and if I was dry, relief would flood me. Most of the time I'd lie there feeling the soaking wetness of the sheets and my pajamas and dreading the coming minutes. Each time I'd feel like crying. Why was I wet when I tried so hard not to be? The scolding words would come, "You've done it on purpose. Fran, you're a big girl now. This wetting has got to stop."

It was with gladness when the days of the Children's Home came to an end. However, the first foster home I went to only lasted a short time. Children who wet the bed weren't wanted there. With a feeling of shame I left that house and went onto the next one.

Finally a home for all four of us was found in the country, not far from a town called Issaquah. The second month we were there something glorious occurred. I remember so clearly the foster mother saying, "Your mother's coming to visit you today." I jumped up and down. Mama was coming! I told Dottie the good news, but she didn't understand. She'd forgotten who her mother was.

The three of us older ones waited the morning and most of the afternoon. Then, finally, there was a knock at the door. Mama came in, a little uncertain at first, her

eyes resting on the four of us across the room in the doorway. Linda and Fred held back but I raced to her and
threw my arms about her. She sat gingerly on the edge of
the scratchy mohair sofa and rocked me on her lap and
patted my head. To me she smelled good and familiar
like the bottles I remembered under her bed.

She held out her arms to the others and they came,
too. For those few minutes I was so happy even my toes
tingled with pleasure.

Too soon the visit was over and as soon as she was
gone Linda spoke bitterly, "She was drunk. Why did she
have to be drunk when she came to see us?" Linda cried
herself to sleep that night and I didn't understand why.

One time when Mama came I was prepared with a
surprise for her. After she'd greeted us, I whispered, "Do
you want to hear me count?" She said she did. Standing
right beside her with all of her attention focused on me I
began, "One, two, three . . . " and went all the way up to
"ninety-nine, one-hundred."

Mother clasped her hands together. "Oh, Fran,
s'wonderful, s'wonderful." It didn't matter to me that she
was drunk and the words of praise were slurred. I had
had my mother's full attention and had received her approval. It was the only time that had ever happened, and
those few minutes remain the greatest moment of my
childhood.

The next foster home was both sad and happy, sad
because Mama wasn't allowed to visit us any longer, happy because our new foster mother was a wonderfully
warm woman. The house seemed big to us, and there
were lots of other children there, even a parrot, a pet rac-
coon and a donkey. Our foster father loved us and
carved us dollhouse furniture from scrap lumber.

Once when I woke up soaking wet I wouldn't get out
of bed. My foster mother came upstairs and lifted me on
her lap, wet pajamas and all, "Don't be sad, Honey, you
won't always wet the bed. The problem will go away
someday."

Twelve years later I visited the house and couldn't

believe how small and ramshackled it was. I could see that my foster father could probably have worked at repairs and paint instead of carving wooden toys, but as a child I experienced nothing but the warmth of those two people.

They took me to the Baptist church and it was there I had an experience with God. I was sitting next to the wall in the children's Sunday school, while in the next room the adults attended church. Over the sound of the children's lesson came the most beautiful song I'd ever heard. I put my ear to the wall and heard the words, "Softly and tenderly Jesus is calling . . . calling to you."

By now I was eight years old and my little eight-year-old heart stirred at those words. I knew I was being called by Jesus.

I told no one but I treasured that moment and never forgot it. Ahead of me lay much perversion, perversion that Jesus knew would happen, and yet he called me. Today, it still amazes me to think how limitless His love is.

I know that foster mother would have kept us if she'd been able, but she became ill, and so the four of us were moved again. We stayed in many homes. Sometimes the bedwetting was a real problem and sometimes the foster mothers understood that it wasn't done on purpose.

Some of the foster parents were loving but others were rushed and cranky. How could they know I longed to be hugged and loved far more than I wanted to be clean and seated in front of a warm dinner.

One of our foster homes had an adopted daughter the same age as Dottie. Both girls had the same name, Dorothy. My Dorothy had to change her name, and that is how we came to call her Dottie. Dottie and I always felt that their Dorothy was liked the best. When both girls had the measles their Dorothy got to stay in the Sunday parlor while Dottie had to stay in the everyday room. Their Dorothy got to stay in when it was wet, but we had to go outside and play anyway.

Once, in a fit of anger, Dottie scratched Dorothy with

14

her fingernails. Our foster mother was furious. Without warning she scratched Dottie from her shoulder to her wrist with her own fingernails. Dottie screamed and ran to me, ribbons of skin hanging from her arm and blood running down her hands. I hugged Dottie and tried to protect her. Together Dottie and I hated that woman more than anything.

I stayed the longest with foster parents by the name of Schmidt. Mr. and Mrs. Schmidt had lived in Germany and their ways were still as old country as their thick German accents. They owned a dairy farm with orchards and vineyards and fields of hay and alfalfa. They had applied to the foster care agency for one little girl Dottie's age, but the caseworker had talked them into taking the four of us. It wasn't the most ideal situation.

The first day when I sat my little dolls in a row and began to teach them school, Mrs. Schmidt laughed loudly, "You play wit doll? Josef, come here, look this big girl, she play wit dolls."

"Baby stuff," Mr. Schmidt laughed scornfully. "Dolls ist for babies."

I wanted to die from embarrassment. I wanted approval so much that I couldn't stand to have anyone ridicule me. I put the dolls back in their brown paper sack and never took them out again.

I could never make up my own mind about whether or not I liked a foster home. With each home I would ask Linda, "Do you like it?" If she did, then I would like it, too. If she didn't, well, neither did I. After a couple of days at the Schmidts I asked if she liked it there.

She shook her head, "No, I don't like it here at all. The Schmidts are the weirdest people we've stayed with yet."

One of the "weird" things about Mrs. Schmidt was her affection for her dog, Hans. While we children slept on a screened porch even in the freezing winter months, Hans slept in a crib right beside Mrs. Schmidt's bed. She covered him with a quilt at night and talked to him as if he could understand her. She worried over his health more than if he were a baby.

All of us learned how to please the Schmidts. The first week we were there, two cords of wood were dumped in the back yard. While the Schmidts were in town Linda, who was now fourteen; Fred, who was twelve; me, at ten, and Dottie, who was eight, all worked feverishly to get it split and piled against the house.

The Schmidts had scorned my dolls, but they heartily approved of hard work. They pulled into the driveway and looked with amazement at what we'd accomplished. "Goot," Mr. Schmidt said, "that was goot. You work hard, you are goot children." We beamed at his approval. Even though I had been working at a hard and fast pace for several hours and was bone weary, the approval of these new foster parents was worth it all.

So began a new era, a time of learning to work very hard. Eagerly, I set about learning to milk the cows so I could win approval of these people. Before I knew it the four of us had become the farm hands, milking the cows each morning at 5:30 a.m. and cleaning up after them.

Linda continued to be dissatisfied with our new foster home. Partly she may have been afraid of the hired man, partly the work was hard, but partly she rebelled against the old-fashioned way of the Schmidts who allowed us children no privileges at all. For one thing Mr. and Mrs. Schmidt went to bed just after supper, and we were expected to do the same. A month after we moved there Linda whispered to Fred and me after we were settled in our beds, "I'm not staying here any longer. I've got to get away."

I shivered under the covers. "Linda, don't go," I cried. "Don't leave me, Linda." I could bear Mama being gone, but not Linda. She was the one I looked to for everything.

"I've got to go, Fran. I can't stay. I hate it too much." Linda may have been fourteen on the outside but on the inside, experience had made her far older.

On a Sunday afternoon Fred and Linda and I sneaked out the open window on the porch with Linda's baggage. I was so scared my knees shook as we cautiously edged our way past the house and barn. Once we were in the woods we ran as fast as we could. Down the hill we went, across the fields, and over the highway until we came to the bus stop. Huffing and puffing we huddled together waiting for the bus to come.

I hugged Linda tightly and she kissed me goodbye. A tear slid down her face and landed on my cheek. She pushed me away, "Hurry up and get home before you get in trouble." I put my hand in Fred's and we fled back over the road, up the hill and through the woods. All I could think was that Linda was going out of my life, too. Fred and I wept all the way back without her.

Chapter 3

When Linda's absence was discovered, Fred and I were interrogated over and over. "Fran, where is she?" our caseworker asked.

"I don't know, honest."

"Fred, where was she going?"

"I don't know."

"Come on," the caseworker demanded, "You do know. Both of you know and you're not telling."

"No, we don't; just leave us alone."

On and on the questioning went. Mr. Schmidt would add his dire predictions, "Dat no goot sister of yours is going to go to reform school. You joost vait til they catch her, you'll be sorry you help."

The truth, of course, was that neither Fred nor I had any idea what might have happened to Linda. The nights were often long as we wondered between ourselves and hoped she was okay.

The greatest problem of all of being at the Schmidts was the hired man. He was about forty, nice looking, I remember, but way too friendly. One afternoon when Dottie and I were helping with chores in the barn, he

18

started kidding around. "I wonder how much you girls weigh. Let me just guess."

"Guess me first," I begged.

"Hmmm, it's hard to tell. Let me feel how much meat you have on those arms." I held out my arms and he felt them but he didn't stop there. He felt my legs and then ran his hands over my body. He was friendly and always smiling. "Well, I'd say you're about 65 pounds. Do you agree with that?"

"Okay."

"Then here's a candy bar for you." Then he turned to Dottie. "How about you?"

"Nope," Dottie said, "not me." She backed away. I thought she was taking a foolish chance. Why would she want to risk the disapproval of anyone who was friendly towards us? Just as long as I had this man's approval it didn't matter to me that he touched my body and even made me feel strange inside. He made a great production out of the breeding of the bull and a cow. "Now there's something coming up that I don't want you and Dottie to see," he'd tell us, "don't you look. It's not a nice thing for girls. Turn your backs and close your eyes." Of course, we were all the more curious about what was going on and went to great lengths to see this thing we shouldn't see.

Breeding time always made him act strangely. I came to expect he'd want to play the how-much-do-you-weigh game after each breeding session. I was too young to understand why, and there wasn't a soul on earth I could talk to about the way he always wanted to touch my body.

Meanwhile, the bed wetting continued to be a problem. Mrs. Schmidt had little patience. "Such a large girl," she ridiculed, "too lazy to get out da warm bed and go to da toilet." She put a portable toilet in the hall so I wouldn't have to go downstairs. "Now use da toilet and no more playing da lazy girl." If I woke up I used it but most of the time, to my embarrassment, in the morning I was wet. Many mornings a week I went off to school with her scoldings ringing in my ears.

With Linda gone I longed to get away from the farm, too. I missed my previous foster mother very much and it occurred to me that she might be missing me as much as I missed her. I believed that she was out looking for me, and I set out to help her find me.

Day after day, I stood on the road, my blonde hair stringing in my eyes, my brown, tweed, hand-me-down coat hanging open over a faded farm dress. Car after car passed by. Eagerly, I scanned each face until, at last, I was sure I saw her.

"Mama," I hollered. "Mama, it's me, Fran." The car kept going. At the top of my lungs I screamed after it, "Ma-maa." Tears slipped down my face before I decided that maybe that wasn't her after all. There were many days, lonely days, pain-filled days, that I called after cars that never stopped.

Meanwhile, I turned eleven and the hired man had a new game. "Fran, would you do me a favor?" he asked in his friendliest voice.

Always trying to please, I answered, "Sure."

"Would you come over to the big sink in the dairy house in a few minutes and scrub my back while I take a bath."

"Okay." Gladly I went and gladly I scrubbed his back. I did it every week for him. It didn't take too long to get used to seeing him naked. While I scrubbed, he talked.

"You know what the most wonderful thing in the world is, Fran?"

"No, what is it?"

"Sex."

"You mean when the bull and the cow ... "

"Yes, but with people. It's great. You really should try it. It would be a good experience for you. No one should get married unless they've tried sex first ... " On and on he talked.

A year had gone by since the day Linda had left, and for that whole time the longing for her in my heart never ceased. I thought of her more than I ever thought of my mother. Every good happening, every "A" paper, everything fun was dulled because Linda wasn't there. Every miserable thing was intensified. There was no one I could go to. Mrs. Schmidt might make fun of me. Fred had his own pain to deal with, since Mr. Schmidt was extremely hard on him. Dottie was too little. I wondered constantly where Linda was and if she was safe or if she might even be dead.

It was at dinner time that the news came. Mr. Schmidt was sitting at the head of the table, buttering his bread. "Dat no goot sister of yours is back."

"Linda!" My heart skipped. "Where is she?"

"The detention home. Where do you think? Dat's where girls like her go."

I paid no attention to the negatives. Linda was safe. She wasn't dead. I'd see her again. My heart sang all through dinner. Later I found out she'd caught a bus going to Chicago. She'd lied about her age, gotten a job and had been taken in by some good people. But she'd missed us, Fred and Dottie and me, and had come back to be with us. Instead, she'd been picked up and placed in detention. Detention or not, I felt happy knowing where she was.

It was about that time that the hired man began talking to me about his previous marriage. One morning while I was squatting on the milk stool, still half asleep, milking the cows he paused by my stall and said, "You know why my marriage failed, Fran?"

"No."

"Because of sex. My wife, she didn't believe in sex. Believe me, all women should know what sex is about before marriage. Then they'll know if they want to get married or not." He smiled, "Isn't that right, Fran?"

"Sure, I guess so."

"Well, Fran, I hope somebody comes along and teaches you about sex before you get married. It would be doing you a big favor."

In the early morning with Fred and Dottie milking at one end of the barn and me and the hired man at the other end, that conversation would get repeated over and over.

That year, the year I turned eleven something else happened, too, to add to the uncertainties of my life. Once again we were all at the table, the Schmidts, Fred, Dottie, me and the hired man. Mrs. Schmidt spoke to Dottie. "Honey, Mr. Schmidt and I vant to adopt you. Ve vant a little girl joost your age and joost as goot as you."

Dottie beamed, "You'll be my own mom and dad and I'll always live here?"

The Schmidts both smiled, "Our own goot little girl."

Suddenly, I felt cold and so scared that my spoon clattered to the floor. I wanted to scream, "What about me? What's going to happen to me?" I knew that Fred was restless and wasn't going to be around much longer. Dottie would belong to the Schmidts. Where would I go? What would I do? Tears came to my eyes and I pushed them away before Mrs. Schmidt could jeer at them.

For the first time in a long time all I could think of was that I wanted my own mother. I didn't care what she was or what she was doing. I didn't care if she was drunk. More than anything else in the world I wanted to belong to somebody. I excused myself and went out to the barn. Throwing myself on the hay, I let the tears fall.

Later the hired man said, "Come on, Fran, I know what let's do. Let's see how much you weigh." Listlessly, I let him play his game. Afterward he offered me a cigarette instead of a candy bar. Willingly, I took it.

If the Schmidts had been more modern in their thinking and more understanding of me and my needs, I think things still could have worked out okay. But they had one philosophy and I had another. Theirs was that children must work. Play was wrong. No one should waste time on foolishness.

My philosophy was to be accepted, to do whatever you had to do to win the approval of others. I had reached an age where it was especially important to have the approval of my friends at school. Specifically, I felt I could win this approval if I could just go to the baseball games everyone else went to in the evenings.

I figured dinner would be as good a place as any to ask. "Mr. Schmidt, can I go to the baseball game in town tonight?"

"Baseball game! Mama, you hear dat? She vants to vaste time at a baseball game."

"Please, oh please. Everyone else in the sixth grade is going."

Those were the wrong words.

"Everyvun else. Ha! Ve are not like everyvun else, vasting time wit games. Ve vork. Vork is goot. Ve do not go to baseball; ve go to bed early and ve get up early and ve do not play. Now you try to be goot like your sister, Dottie, and don't be always making da trouble."

Across the table the hired man winked at me and motioned toward the barn. I met him there after dinner. "I'll take you," he said, "as soon as the old lady is in bed."

He did take me and even bought me popcorn. I sat with my friends and he brought me home afterwards. By now I was twelve and I was wise. I knew he'd want to play how-much-do-you-weigh. I didn't care. Getting to the game with my friends from school was much more important.

Only I was wrong about his game. He didn't mention it. Instead he had another plan. He'd heard about something he wanted me to do with him.

"Just take off your clothes."

"No, please don't make me."

"Let me see what you look like."

"No, please."

"Do you want me to tell Schmidt you went to the baseball game?"

"Oh, no, please don't."

"Then you will do what I ask?"

My voice was so low, I couldn't hear it myself, "Unhuh." I did what he wanted. I felt dirty; more than that, I felt trapped. There was no way out.

23

I learned that if I did it without thinking too much about it, it wasn't too bad. I'd already vowed that I'd never go all the way with him. If these other things he wanted me to do got me time with my friends I'd just do them and not dwell on it. It never occurred to me to tell anyone what was going on. I was sure I was as guilty as he was in Mr. Schmidt's eyes for going to the baseball games.

At the same time I devised a scheme to get rid of the hired man. "Mrs. Schmidt," I'd say, "the hired man spilled a whole bucket of milk and cleaned it up so you wouldn't know about it." "Mrs. Schmidt, the hired man says your dog, Hans, is a stupid mutt." Or I'd reverse things and say to the hired man, "Mrs. Schmidt says you're slow as molasses. She says you walk like a chicken." Hopefully, pitting them against each other would get rid of him before anything worse happened in the barn.

Although Mr. Schmidt often made fun of me, I knew he admired me. I was sure of that because I worked hard winning that admiration. The work on the farm was end-less. In addition to the barn work, in the spring I worked beside him cutting the grape vines and getting the ground ready for planting. In the summer, I worked all day cutting hay. Fall and early winter meant more long hours harvesting the apples and grapes. Mr. Schmidt had his own reward system: a little glass of homemade wine for a good day's work. Seven-Up and wine on Sunday after-noon, beer in the middle of the day during haying season.

It didn't matter that I was a child. In the old country it was permissible for children to have beer and wine. I started looking forward to that wine at the end of the day. Before long I was drinking it whenever I got the chance.

Looking back, I don't know why the Schmidts weren't more aware of what was going on out in the barn. Did they know and just close their eyes? Or did they trust the hired man without question? I've since learned that many, many adults have been blind to what was happening to their young girls and boys. They trusted family friends, uncles, stepfathers, foster fathers, half brothers, even natural fathers without even questioning what might be going on when their backs were turned. A web was spun around the children, and their own guilt and participation made it impossible for them to break away. It was into that kind of a situation that I found myself locked.

Since I had no family ties, my school friends formed the most important relationships of my life. Those times we spent were so innocent and the price was so great. Eventually, the hired man had me doing what I vowed I'd never do.

"Come on, Fran, I'm just going to show you what sex is like. You'll love it."

"No, I don't want to."

"Come on, sit beside me and we'll have a cigarette."

I accepted the cigarette gratefully. I was getting to the point of needing them. I smoked it clear down to the butt.

"How about another cigarette?"

"Sure."

"Well, first let me just show you what you need to know."

"But I don't want to."

"Come on, Fran."

"No."

"The play-off game is Friday night."

"No, please."

"Fran, I promise you'll love it."

I hated it. It wasn't anything good at all. It made me want to cry and cry inside.

The pattern was begun.

At the dinner table he'd wink one eye, and I knew I had to meet him that night after the others were asleep. I drank enough wine ahead of time to somehow endure it. For months I told no one.

I did intensify the cold war between him and the Schmidts. At long last he was fired and I was

free. Shortly after that my first period started and I
turned thirteen.

Chapter
4

"Dottie, you wet the bed," I shook her awake. "Now you can be the one to change the sheets."

She rolled over and growled, "I did not and you know it. You're the one who did it."

"I didn't either." It was an old argument, both of us trying to put the guilt on the other. I'd awakened that morning and felt the familiar feeling of being soaked all over. I was fourteen and more ashamed than ever to still be wetting. Naturally, I blamed Dottie. The shame was so great I couldn't bear to accept it.

Ignoring me, Dottie went back to sleep. I lay there in the Schmidt's cold, screened-porch bedroom, thinking how I would have given anything to be dry. I thought of my various friends at school. I was certain that they couldn't possibly have accidents at night. Envy washed over me, envy that my friends weren't wet in the morning and I was. No one knew how I hated myself each time I awoke to the bitterly personal failure of wetting the bed.

It had been a little over a year since the hired man had been fired and his replacement was an older man who gladly gave us cigarettes without asking for favors. Fred had been sent to a different foster home and even though I missed him I knew he was happier being elsewhere than at the Schmidts.

I'd heard from Linda. She'd run away from the detention home, met a fellow named Lee and gotten married. They lived in Montana and her letters sounded truly happy. I missed her; the ache in my heart for Linda was always there, but at the same time I was glad for her.

My life had taken an interesting turn. Even though I wasn't a part of the "in" group at school, the way every girl longs to be, I had discovered the neighborhood boys. Or maybe it was the other way--they discovered me.

Dale was sixteen and handsome. He had broad shoulders and blond hair. His eyes were deep set and blue. I imagined that perhaps my dad, whom I'd never even seen a picture of, must have looked like him. Dale paid a lot of attention to me and I loved being important to him.

I was getting a nice rounded figure. My blonde hair was easy to curl and I even wore a little lipstick. Everyone still said my eyes were my best feature. One afternoon Dale said, as he usually did, "Fran, get some of old man Schmidt's wine and meet us at the shack across from the barn tonight."

"Sure," I promised. The Schmidts had so much wine -- they made it in fifty gallon barrels -- they never missed what I took to share with my friends.

I had a full bottle when I met Dale and several others. I sat down beside him in the hay that was stacked in the shack. "Got a cigarette?" I asked. I'd gone since morning without one and I could barely stand it. He offered me one and I lit it quickly, cupping my hand around the match like the expert I'd become. I inhaled deeply, holding the smoke as long as I could and then blowing it in the air with the nonchalance I knew the boys admired in me. I was the only girl around who really smoked.

We had one cup for all of us. I poured it full. Dale

drank about half and passed it to the others. Between the rest of them they finished it. I poured myself a full cup and downed it all. I could see the surprise and admiration on the faces of Dale's friends. I poured another full cup and downed it as quickly. I'd been drinking at the end of a long day's work since I was eleven so two cups of wine was nothing for me. I passed the cup around again and downed a third cup when it came back to me.

We smoked some more and Dale sat closer to me, his arm around my waist. Then his hand slid under my sweater and unfastened my bra. I kissed him with a kiss that said it was okay. The many experiences with the hired man had conditioned me to accept the direction that fellows always wanted to go. Only now I wasn't being coerced. I longed for the approval of this boy who might even look like my father.

After a little more wine went around, Dale's friends left. We laid on the hay and kissed over and over. I loved the feeling of being in his arms. His searching hands felt familiar. His eager body didn't startle me. At the end of the evening he probably thought of me as a conquest. I was probably even more pleased at being able to arouse him so thoroughly.

With this new experience came a new fear. Month after month if my period was even a few hours late I would start to worry that I was pregnant. I'd whisper to Dottie as we lay in bed at night, "What will we do, Dottie, if I'm going to have a baby?"

"We do!" she whispered back. "If you're pregnant, it's your problem."

"I mean would you run away with me so the caseworker wouldn't find us?"

"Sure I would. Would you keep the baby?"

"Oh, yes." Tears came to my eyes. "Oh, if I had a baby I'd love it and take care of it and never, never leave it alone. If I had a baby I would never even drink again . . ."

Sometimes Dottie and I would whisper about Mama. "Where do you think she is?" I'd ask. "Why do you suppose she's never contacted us?"

Dottie hardly remembered her so she didn't care as much as I did. "Well, at least we know she's not dead. If she was dead the Schmidts would have adopted me by now but they can't do it unless she dies or gives her consent."

I repeated the comforting thought. "Yes, she's not dead or we'd know. She's busy. Very busy and she lives somewhere else." Once more the longing for my mother welled up in me until I thought I would die of it. Where could she be? Why hadn't she ever written to us?"

The day my first period had started I'd missed her terribly. I knew about menstruation from Linda, but I wasn't ready for the shock of it happening to me. I stood there alone in the cold bathroom and awkwardly fastened the necessary paraphernalia. I wanted my mother, I needed her there. Just to have her tell me that what was happening to my body was really okay would have meant more than anything.

I missed her when it came to even littler things like body odor. Mr. Schmidt's younger brother, Fritz, who was a "city man" took me aside one day, "Fran, when girls reach your age their bodies start giving off unpleasant underarm odors. What you need to do is go to the drugstore and buy some *Mum* and use it under your arms everyday before you go to school."

I was deeply embarrassed over that conversation and even more embarrassed at the drugstore. I just couldn't seem to bring myself to buy anything so personal. I stalled at the perfume counter and stalled some more over the baby powder. The druggist finally asked, "Can I help you?"

"Uh, uh, yes, I mean no, I mean, I'm just looking." I decided to leave and come back with Dottie and make her buy it. I couldn't do that, though. Fritz said I shouldn't go to school without it. I walked over to the Band-aids and stared at them for a long time. Finally I got the courage to make my purchase.

I bought the large 39 cent jar so I wouldn't have to buy

it again for a long time. Walking home I thought of Mama. I wasn't bitter or resentful. I just wished she'd been there to buy the *Mum* for me.

Another summer came, followed by another winter of rising each morning in the cold and going to the barn for chores. Finally April with its relative warmth arrived. By now I was fifteen and finishing my sophomore year in high school. It was late Saturday afternoon when I burst into the kitchen after the evening milking, starved and ready for dinner. The kitchen was empty, the stove cold. I had always been able to count on Mrs. Schmidt's bustling figure preparing the evening meal. Where could she be? A sudden chill raced through me. I ran up the stairs to the bedroom and flung open the door. "Mrs. Schm ..."

She was lying on her bed, unable to speak, her eyes staring straight ahead. She wasn't dead; somehow I knew that, but I couldn't have been more scared. I sprinted to the neighbors to use their telephone. Mr. Schmidt came right away and, shortly after, the doctor arrived. When all the commotion died down, we were told that she'd had a massive stroke.

That night Dottie and I had something exciting to whisper about. Linda had been allowed to have Fred come and live with her and Lee, and she'd tried to get us girls, too, but the authorities had turned down her request for us.

"Wouldn't it be wonderful," I whispered, "if we could go to Linda's in Montana?"

"Do you think we really could?" Wistfulness hung to Dottie's every word.

A month went by and then another one while the case worker tried to find us a home in Washington state. Then one gray, rainy, June day I picked up the mail and there was a letter from the State of Washington. Rain drizzled over my face as I stood on the water-soaked road and ripped open the envelope. Then I was screaming, "Dottie, Dottie, it's here, it's here. Guess what? We're going to Linda's."

31

So ended five hard years with the Schmidts. I'd come at ten years of age, innocent and vulnerable. I was leaving hooked on cigarettes, leaning on alcohol and painfully knowledgeable of the ways of men. I'd come with a need to be loved and accepted, and I was leaving with that same need unmet.

Our train arrived in Great Falls, Montana, at 11:30 in the morning. Outside the window we could see Fred, Linda, her husband Lee, and their baby Randy. Dottie and I grabbed our suitcases and raced to the end of the car so we could be the first ones off. "Watch your step," the porter called, but we were down the stairs before the words were finished.

I got to her first. "Linda!" It was so good to put my arms around her, to touch, to look at her. Linda!

I hugged Fred and Lee and little Randy and then hugged Linda again. I stood back and looked at each face and thought how wonderful we all looked, a family standing together in the brilliant Montana sunlight.

Linda and Lee's house was typical of many Montana houses that had once been one room and had been gradually added onto. There were four rooms in a row, a kitchen, a living room and two bedrooms. You had to go through one to get to the other. It was crowded to say the least, but Linda had the sleeping all arranged, Fred on the sofa in the living room; Dottie and I in the little bedroom in the middle and Linda and Lee and the baby in the back bedroom. Fred kept his things in with Dottie's and mine, and somehow we worked it all out.

Linda had planned a picnic for us. We all drove in Lee's old sedan until we came to a place in the mountains Linda had picked out in advance. It was perfect. A stream gurgled by, tall trees shaded us, pine needles provided a rich carpet for our blankets. Baby Randy settled down to sleep in his car bed under a low fir tree. Linda, Fred, Dottie, Lee and I settled down to talk and talk some more. I felt so free, so-lighthearted, as if every trouble and every pain had melted away. I felt certain that true happiness was finally beginning for all of us now that we were with each other again.

Linda opened a picnic basket and passed around chicken sandwiches, potato salad, pickles, potato chips and chocolate chip cookies. Lee poured Kool-aid in paper cups and handed one to me. I took it even though it was somewhat of a surprise. Fred was sitting beside me and I asked him in a low voice, "Isn't there any beer?"

He shook his head. "Linda doesn't allow it. Lee doesn't believe in alcoholic beverages, it's something to do with his religion."

Hmmm, that was interesting. No beer or wine at the end of the day would be quite a switch for Dottie and me since we'd been drinking it for so long. But it didn't matter. The most important thing in the whole world was pleasing Linda. I didn't need anything more than just being with her again.

At Linda's house bedwetting wasn't the problem it had been. If I were wet I washed the sheets myself. Linda never commented on it and her attitude kept me from getting down on myself. Since it was only happening once a month or less, I began to think that someday it might stop altogether.

The only thing I dreaded was starting eleventh grade in the fall. Always, starting a new school was painful. Even though I eventually made a few friends, I had never belonged to the "in" crowd. The teachers all knew me as somebody's foster child and before long the kids thought of me that way, too. When the popular girls planned their parties I was always on the outside, hearing about them but never invited.

I knew Great Falls High School would be no different. The first week of school it was easy to pick out the popular girls. I could tell by the way they walked and talked, even by the way they tossed their heads when they laughed. They had a certain way of wearing their clothes that made what I wore seem out of place to me. I sat in my classes and looked at them from afar, envying their popularity.

One of these girls, Patty, sat across from me in

Biology. One Friday afternoon she casually asked, "Fran, do you want to go bowling with a few of us girls tonight?"

Did I? More than she could ever guess. "Sure." I made my voice nonchalant as if the most popular girls invited me to go with them all the time.

She said to meet the others at the Dew Drop Inn Bowling Alley at 7:00 p.m.

I nearly floated home from school. I washed my hair, set it in pincurls and then went to the kitchen to tell Linda the good news. "Guess what! I've been invited to go bowling with some of the neatest girls in school."

Linda was enthusiastic, "That's great. Fran, I'm glad you're making friends."

It was so wonderful that night not to sneak out like I'd always done at the Schmidts but to say good-bye to the family and have them call out, "Have a good time."

The girls who were there were the ones I'd already picked out as the "in" group. We laughed and told jokes and I couldn't remember having more fun. There was no embarrassment in saying that I was staying with my sister like there had been in saying I lived in a foster home.

After bowling we went to one of the girl's houses. "Come on," she invited, "my folks aren't home." She casually put a couple dozen bottles of beer on the kitchen table and the other girls helped themselves. I could tell they were waiting to see what I'd do. I thought of Linda and how she didn't want me to drink, but even as I thought of it my hand was reaching for a bottle. Expertly, I uncapped it with the opener, downed it and reached for another one.

As I reached for a third, I saw the open admiration in the eyes of the girls I wanted to impress. I gulped it down and reached for a fourth. My alcohol tolerance was so high I wasn't even close to being drunk. That night the miracle of popularity happened to me. I had become a part of the crowd that was "in."

It was about a month later that Linda asked me to come outside and sit on the steps with her. We talked about how beautiful Montana is in the autumn and how good it was to be together. Then Linda got to the point. "Fran, I hear you're running with a fast crowd. I hope this doesn't mean you're drinking. I know the kids in Montana drink a lot."

"I drink a little," I admitted, "but it's no big deal."

"Fran, I'm going to have to ask you not to drink at all. Lee doesn't want either you or Dottie to drink. Dottie has been going around with kids who drink, too, but I'm sure if you quit so will she."

"I'll try," I told her. I wanted to make Linda happy. "I really will. And I'll talk to Dottie, too."

Linda hugged me. "Thanks for understanding."

She went in the house and I sat on the steps and planned how the next time we went bowling I'd refuse to have a beer. I could picture myself saying, "No, I don't drink anymore."

But the next time I was with my friends I did what they expected of me. I outdrank everyone without even feeling dizzy.

I knew what Linda was going to say even before she opened her mouth. She had been crabby all evening and I was sure I knew why. It was 10:00 p.m. Lee had gone to bed, Dottie was babysitting for the neighbor. Fred had just left a few days before for the Navy so there were only the two of us sitting at the kitchen table over hot mugs of coffee. "Fran, I've got to talk to you about your drinking."

"Well, what about it?"

"It hasn't stopped, has it?"

"What if it hasn't?" Almost belligerently I defended myself, "And I don't see anything wrong with it, either."

Linda was angry for the first time, "Fran, it's wrong because I asked you not to do it. What's going on with you that you can't obey me?"

Suddenly, I was angry, too. Linda was my mother, my friend, my ally. But now she seemed like just another cold, impersonal counselor and for the first time I felt hurt by her. My life was going so well, why was she trying to ruin it all?

"Fran, I'm upset with you that you haven't kept your promise to me. If you girls don't stop it, I won't allow either one of you to stay here. Lee feels it's wrong to drink."

I could hardly believe my ears. I just stared at her. Since when had Lee become more important to her than Dottie and me? We'd been her family long before she knew him.

"Please, Fran, don't you understand how important this is to Lee?"

Lee! A coldness passed through me.

What a traitor she'd turned out to be. I could almost hate her. As icily as I could I said, "Okay, if that's the way you want it, if you want to ruin my whole life, then that's fine with me." I dumped the coffee in the sink and went past her to bed without saying goodnight.

I didn't sleep, I was too angry. What right did she have to tell me how to live my life? I felt utterly betrayed. Then I was crying. I couldn't bear to lose my friends and I'd surely lose them if I didn't drink. I couldn't bear to lose Linda either.

Chapter 5

I met him in a restaurant where I was a waitress. Bob, a soldier at the Air Force Base outside of town, was tall, blond like I was, and his eyes were kind and soft. He told me I was the sweetest, most wonderful girl he'd ever known.

For the first time in my life I knew what it was like to be in love. The problem was that Linda didn't approve of my dating a soldier. She didn't mind if I dated the boys at school, but to me they seemed unbearably young and immature. Despite the fact that she had run away from the Schmidt's at fourteen, had been in detention and married at sixteen, she had never done anything wrong with boys or men. She was determined to keep my life as clean as she had kept hers.

I'd sit at my desk at school and agonize. I didn't want to sneak out or lie, but what could I do? I wanted Bob but I didn't want to hurt Linda. Why was Linda so strict? Why couldn't she understand? Why did Bob have to mean so much to me? Bob or Linda? Who did I choose?

Linda was getting tough with me; Bob loved and accepted me just the way I was. In the end I chose him. Before I knew it I was back to the old habits of sneaking out and lying, only this time I was lying to someone who loved me. Gone was the good feeling of being honest that I'd had in the beginning with Linda and her husband.

Bob could get whiskey on the Air Force base so we parked in his car up in the hills and drank and smoked and talked half the night. During this time Linda thought I was either babysitting or with the girls.

One still Montana night Bob and I watched the moon rise through the pine trees, and I told him about my mother and how I hoped I would see her someday.

He was older, and in his wisdom and love for me he advised, "Fran, I don't think you'll ever see her again. Don't build yourself up for something that will never happen."

We sat for a while in silence while I considered his words. Finally I said, "Bob, I have to believe I'll find her. I have to for her sake. I know she misses me as much as I miss her."

"Fran, honey, don't count on it, okay?" He encouraged me not to get my hopes up for something he thought was impossible.

I told him about Linda and how our friendship was strained, and he seemed to share the pain I felt over it all. He took me in his arms and said he understood.

At home, Dottie and I continued our whispering after the lights were out. Almost from the time I met Bob I began to worry that I was pregnant. I shared this worry with Dottie. Each month when I'd find out I was "safe," she'd say, "Fran, why don't you just tell these guys no?"

"I couldn't do that?"

"Why not?"

"Because it's as important to me as it is to them."

Just as I'd won the attention of the girls at school with drinking, I'd won the attention of Bob and other fellows with sex. It didn't seem one bit wrong to me. I'd learned early that sex was a part of the package when a boy was around.

In February Bob was sent to Korea. I missed him terribly. More than anybody in the world, he'd treated me tenderly. I walked alone to the edge of town where we'd once walked together. The tears fell because I loved him and he was gone. I found myself crying, crying for myself, for my mother, then for all of us kids, and for all the trouble I'd ever known.

In school the most popular girls were on the basketball team, so, of course, I joined, too. It helped to take up the time I had on my hands now that Bob was gone. We ended each game, win or lose, with a beer bust. I could still drink more than any of the others.

One night Linda was waiting up for me. I came in and found her sitting straight up on the sofa. Her eyes met mine and practically bore holes in me. Disgust filled her voice, "You smell like a bar."

"So what?" I snarled.

Linda was furious, "Darn you, Fran, you and Dottie have got to quit drinking or you can't stay here. I've told you that." She was almost yelling, "Why don't you listen to me? Why don't you do as I ask?"

She made me so mad I could have spit at her. What right did she have to turn on me?

"Why can't you just accept me the way I am? Why all the rules and regulations?"

"Fran," she was pleading with me, "These rules are for your own good. You girls have got to follow them." Then she was angry again. "I mean it. Do you hear me? You've got to quit drinking."

"All right, I'll quit. I'll tell Dottie to quit. Are you happy now?"

"No, Fran, I'm not happy now but I'll accept that." There were tears in her eyes but I ignored them and walked past her to bed.

Dottie was asleep and I lay beside her with my clothes still on and buried my face in my hands. Tears stung my eyes. I loved Linda and I really wanted to do what she said. I couldn't imagine ever leaving her house.

Besides, I didn't enjoy drinking. I just did it because everyone thought my ability to store it away was so great.

I pulled out a bottle of beer I'd stashed away in the bottom drawer. Dottie woke up while I drank it. I told her what Linda had said and that she wanted us to give up drinking. For a long time that night we talked about all the authority figures in our lives who'd let us down, various foster parents, teachers who'd treated us like we were second-class. There was even our mother who had never written to us, there was the hired man, the Schmidts who had been indifferent to our needs and now Linda. Linda, of all people, who wouldn't understand. Rebellion toward every single one of them filled me with rage.

My drinking doubled. I drank at school in front of my locker and in the halls. My anger included all authority. I'd show the teachers and principal. I'd defy them all. What right did any of them have to tell me how to live my life?

My friends became my only source of happiness. Only when I was with them did I feel carefree and happy. As winter turned into a warm spring, much of our conversation was spent discussing the coming annual event in Great Falls, Round up Day, which was held the first week of May. There'd be a parade and a rodeo in town and, out in the hills, the biggest teen-age blast of the year would take place.

It was understood that I'd ride in the parade. I got a white cowgirl shirt to wear and borrowed boots and a ten-gallon hat. When the big day came, I rented a horse. I'd never felt so proud in my life as I did that day, riding with the others while the people on the street cheered us all.

At the blast afterwards I drank more than I'd ever drunk in my life. I don't remember being dropped off at home, but apparently I went into the bathroom and tried to throw up in the toilet. Without knowing that I'd completely missed the toilet, I went to bed. Lee came home later, walked into the bathroom and found the mess. I woke up with my head aching severely and everything around me looking fuzzy. Through the pain and fuzziness I could hear Lee saying, "That does it. You couldn't show us anymore clearly that you don't want to hang around here any longer." I knew I'd really blown it this time. I knew I could no longer live with Linda and Lee.

What would I do? Go back to Seattle? Even with my throbbing head I knew that wasn't the answer. Desperately, I groped for solutions. Then I hit on one that appeared to make a lot of sense. I'd run away! The more I thought about running away the more I liked it. That would fix Linda. She could worry about where I'd gone just like I'd worried when she ran away.

Later that day Dottie agreed to run away with me. We plotted how we would sit up in chairs instead of going to bed, so we could slip away as soon as the house was quiet. At 11:00 we settled into two straight chairs and began to whisper. The next thing I knew Dottie was shaking me awake. I opened my eyes to see that it was already growing light. We'd fallen asleep! I looked at the clock--4:30.

"It's too late, " Dottie cried. "We've slept too long."

"No, come on. We can't stay here, anyway. Let's get out of here right now."

We slipped out the window and walked up the road. Just as the sun slipped over the horizon, we dashed out of view of Linda's house. Cutting through the back way we arrived at the apartment of two of my friends and spent the weekend in hiding from Linda and Lee.

On Monday Dottie and I went to school as usual without realizing that the whole town had been looking for us and that the police had issued a warrant for our arrest. In the middle of my first period class I was summoned to the counselor's office.

The counselor was pleasant. "Fran, where have you been? Everyone's been worried sick."

I shrugged my shoulders. "At a friend's."

"Why did you run away?"

"I wanted to finish school in Montana."

"I see. Well, could you and Dottie stop by your caseworker's on the way home tonight?"

"What for?"

"She wants to talk to you."

"Are we in trouble?"

"No."

"Are you sure?"

"I promise you. You aren't in any trouble but she does want to talk to you. Will you go?"

"I guess so."

"And bring Dottie?"

"Sure, both of us will go."

She got up from her desk. "Well, that's fine, Fran. I'll see you tomorrow."

Dottie and I were at the caseworker's office by 3:00. "I'm scared," Dottie said. "I know we're in for it."

I assured her, "No, the counselor promised we wouldn't be in any trouble."

By 3:15 both of us were in detention. The caseworker had been furious. "If this is the way you want to play, then we'll play it your way. Your sister is too good for you. From now on you two girls are going to have to toe the mark. From now until school is out you will be allowed out of detention just long enough to go to school. You are to come here directly afterwards. No friends, no parties, no booze, no cigarettes. Is that clear?" What's more we would not be allowed to go back to Linda's.

Dottie was in tears. I was too angry to cry. That double crossing counselor. How I hated her. There wasn't a single adult in the world that could be trusted!

The hours at the detention home were colored dull gray, especially the weekend hours. There was nothing to do, no one to talk to. I spent my time lying on my bed, staring at the ceiling.

One Sunday afternoon as I was lying there thinking, as I often did, about the mess I'd made of my life, I heard the sound of singing floating up the stairwell outside my room. It was the voice of a little retarded girl who lived in the detention home because there was no place else for her to go. The words of her song were sung clearly and with the sweetness of a little child:

"It is no secret what God can do.
What He's done for others, He can do for you."

She sang those words again and again. There, as I lay on my bed with those words hanging in the air, I started to cry. What could God do? What had he done for others? What could He possibly do for me?

That song and its message haunted me for days. What could God do with the mess of my life? I was certain He could do nothing.

Linda came to visit us while we were in detention but I felt so ashamed I couldn't even talk with her. To help break the ice between us she planned a going-away party for the day before we were to leave for Seattle. Dottie invited three of her friends and I invited three of mine. Although I enjoyed my friends, for the whole day I refused to let my eyes meet Linda's. No matter what she said I remained as cold as I could be.

The next day she picked us up and took us to the train depot. We stood on the platform, none of us talking to the other. Part of me wanted to throw my arms around her and tell her I loved her and even tell her I was sorry. But I was too hurt and too proud.

She handed me a brown sack. "Here's some chicken and some sandwiches for your lunch." I took it coldly without looking at her.

The good-bye was hard for her. "Fran, Dottie, oh girls, I'm so sorry it didn't work out . . ."

We walked away and boarded the train without a word. We seated ourselves, refusing to look out the window at her. The train pulled out of the station, leaving behind Great Falls and Linda and our dream of ever being happy together again.

Suddenly we were both sobbing, huge wracking sobs that came from the very core of our souls. Mile after mile our sobbing continued. It was the only way we could express the sorrow and pain that were too deep for words.

Chapter
6

M iss Blackstone, our caseworker, was furious. Dottie
and I saw her from the window as the train pulled
into Union Station in downtown Seattle in the early
morning. She was standing on the wooden platform, her
expression grim, her arms folded. She searched the face
of each passenger, looking for two girls she thought she
was finished with, but who were now being added to the
burden of her heavy caseload.

"We're in for it, " I told Dottie. "Look at her face."

"I wonder what she's going to do with us," Dottie
asked.

"It's no big deal. She'll find us another foster
home. What else can she do?" I played it cool, as much
for Dottie as for myself.

"Watch your step, ladies," the porter intoned. My feet
were like lead as I stepped down from the middle step
and onto the platform. Without even a minute to look
around, I found myself face to face with Miss
Blackstone -- instantly in her custody.

We sat across from her in a two-bit cafe around the corner from the depot. She let us order breakfast before she

44

gave us her "little talk." Dottie and I were both inwardly braced for it, but the announcement that followed it was a total shock.

We heard, "Girls, what a disappointment . . . I'd expected more . . . you failed your sister . . . we've all tried to help you . . ." We only half listened. It was a speech we'd heard before and would probably hear again. And then she said, ". . . and now I have some bad news."

Dottie and I looked at each other. Miss Blackstone continued, "We don't have a foster home for you. There just isn't a home available that will take two runaway teenagers. Sorry, but I'm going to have to put you in detention."

Detention! But that was for the bad kids. We weren't bad; we'd just goofed up a little.

"It's only for a little while, a few days," she assured us.

It didn't take us long to understand that another word for detention is jail. At the detention center, a door locked behind us. All that we had -- our jeans that we loved, our purses, everything -- was stripped away, and in their place we pulled on rough, baggy underwear and a one-size-fits-all house dress. It was so humiliating to be dressed like that I could have died. The door to that room locked behind us and we were in detention, behind bars with a lot of other girls -- prostitutes, petty thieves, runaways -- who looked as saggy-baggy as we did.

I'd never known that days could last so long or that nights could be even longer. I remember standing at the barred windows watching the moon rise over Puget Sound. I could see the stars shining clearly above and see the twinkle of the city lights below. There I was, suspended in the middle with no where to go and nothing to do.

"I wonder what Linda's doing." My thoughts automatically went to her. I shook my head to get rid of any remembrances. I hated her now. She'd tried to run my life and I didn't want to think of her ever again. Instead I wondered about my future. Was there any more to life than this? Was there something besides smoking, drinking, sex and trying to get accepted? There had to be, but I didn't know where or what. I stood for a long time, looking at the outside world through those bars but no answer came.

As days dragged by, I found a new way to deal with that constant nagging need inside me to be accepted. It happened on the occasional times Miss Blackstone would stop to take us out for hamburgers. At the restaurant I said, "Would you excuse me for a minute? I have to go to the restroom." As I went by the cigarette machine, I quickly popped a quarter in and pushed the Lucky Strike button. Hardly missing a step, I grabbed the pack and headed for the restroom. Locked in a cubicle, I transferred all but one of the cigarettes to the hem of my clothes. Safely hidden, I lit up the last cigarette. Pure joy! For two or three luxurious minutes my nicotine starved body could relax, the torture of being without cigarettes momentarily over.

As soon as I got back to the changing room, I pulled the cigarettes out of their hiding place and tucked them in my bra or the hem of my house dress. Inside detention, I signaled the others with my eyes that I had a contraband. One by one after supper, we headed for the showers. Peeling off our clothes, we huddled in the space between the showers and the tiled wall. Eagerly we lit up, inhaling deeply, enjoying the sensation. The usual tell-tale smoke mingled with the steam above us and did not give us away.

"Fran, you're terrific!"

"Fran, I couldn't have gone another day without a cigarette. Thanks."

"Fran, you have more nerve. Wow!"

I grinned. "It's nothing." The acceptance I won through smuggling cigarettes filled an even greater emotional need than my physical need for nicotine.

Although Dottie and I were close, we always seemed to make different sets of friends. Mine were always the older ones and Dottie's were the younger. Even so, we spent time together, talking over our worries and our dreams. "Dottie, you know what I want to do?" I asked her one evening. We pulled two chairs together away from the others.

"Get out of here?"

"Besides that." Both of us wanted out, but there was nowhere to go.

"No, what do you want?"

"I want to be on my own. I want to graduate and get every single adult I know off my back. I want to be free. I don't want to ask anyone permission for anything. If I want to smoke, if I want to drink, if I want a guy, I don't want to hide or have to answer to anyone. And, Dottie, do you know what the best night of my life is going to be?"

"No, what?"

"I'm counting the days, minutes and seconds. It's the night I graduate. I've got a party planned that is better than any party I've ever been to in my life. Guys and booze and dancing all night. I'll be celebrating my freedom."

"Can I come?"

"Yes, and bring every one of your friends."

Miss Blackstone came a few days later with good news and bad news. The good news was that we were getting out of detention. The bad news was that although there still wasn't a foster home for us there was an opening for two girls in the Washington Children's Home. So Dottie and I settled once more into new surroundings -- our twelfth move since we'd left Mother when we were little girls.

We'd been at the Home just a few days when the news was announced that the Home's older girls were being sent to Bible Camp. It was a Salvation Army camp, of all places! Welcoming the challenge, the teen-aged girls from the Children's Home agreed. Camp Lake Boren would never be the same.

Cabin G was settled partially in the woods away from the other cabins. We figured they didn't want us bad girls mingling with the others. Inside, there were two rows of four bunks, each standing opposite the other. I picked a top bunk for myself.

The first day there, three other girls and I hitch-hiked to the closest store. Two girls went to the candy counter and accidentally spilled a box of Milky Ways. With everyone picking them up, the other girl and I went to work. She grabbed a couple of packs of cigarettes and tucked them into her coat pocket. I grabbed a handful more and slid them down my blouse. Pulling my coat over the bulge we left the store before the Milky Ways were back on the shelf.

Back at the camp, we were hiding in the bushes smoking, when the camp counselor, Sister McIntosh, discovered us.

"Girls, what are you doing here? What's all this about? Cigarettes! Don't you know you are disobeying? YOU ARE DISOBEYING. Do you hear me? This is disobedience.

Both her anger and words rolled off us like water gliding over pebbles. We had all been in so much trouble one way or another that Sister McIntosh was just another angry voice.

"Girls, I command you to dump that stuff immediately. Do you hear? Immediately!"

The others looked to me for leadership and I led them by taking another puff on my cigarette.

Sister McIntosh squared her shoulders, turned on her heel and marched off. Sister Whitehall took her place.

Sister Whitehall apparently thought that sports would solve the problem. "Okay, everybody, out on the baseball field," she announced to the eight of us in Cabin G. It was after dinner and most of us were waiting for it to get dark enough to go out for an evening smoke. "Come on, let's get some extra practice so that our cabin will be the best team in the tournament." No one budged.

"Fran, I bet you can really pitch."

I shrugged, thinking, "How silly, a tournament."

She appealed to each one of us, but peer pressure remained the greater force. Even the ones who wanted to play wouldn't go if the others didn't. Sister Whitehall resigned and so did her replacement, Sister Anderson, who was the one who wanted us to sing in rounds.

Sister Anderson was replaced by a girl who was only 18 years old. Her name was Sister Walker, but she told us to call her June. Although we were only two years apart in age, we were worlds apart in experience. There was no way I could have liked her at first glance. She wore the somber clothes of the Salvation Army workers. Her brown hair was brushed back from a scrubbed face that had never known a tint of make-up. She was just not in my league.

Her only redeeming quality in my eyes was that she didn't want to scold, play ball or sing. Instead, she curled up on a lower bunk while I leaned out of a khaki-colored sleeping bag on my top bunk across from her. For hours and hours all of us did nothing but talk and she was an eager listener.

For half the night and all the next day, we regaled her with stories, some of them true, most of them not-so-true. It was in the middle of the following night that I woke up and saw her sitting up in bed. "Why aren't you sleeping?" I asked.

"Frankly, Fran, I'm afraid," she whispered. "With you girls around, I have no idea what will happen to me if I fall asleep."

Moonlight lit the cabin and I could tell from the frightened look on her face that she really had believed every word we'd said. This girl who had shown us nothing but love was shivering with fear. For the first time that I could remember, I felt ashamed.

To try to make up for what we'd done I asked, "Do you want to go for a walk?"

She nodded yes. We walked through the camp, the moonlight making the paths a scene from a black and white movie. Under her gentle prodding, I began to talk about the real Fran, the scared Fran, the lonely Fran. I talked about boys and school and, of course, the most painful thing of all in my life -- the continuing question of what could have happened to my mother and whether I would see her again.

June listened without judging. Even more she accepted me just as I was. It was the first time an authority figure had ever simply accepted me. In gratitude, from that point on I made sure she got 100% cooperation from all of us.

June managed to get a truck and take the Cabin G girls to Mount Rainier for a three-day campout. There, away from the regiment of camp; there, where wild flowers covered the mountainside and waterfalls splashed in the distance; there, without having to use sex or cigarettes or beer to gain favor, I was loved and accepted.

One night as we sat by the fire, smoking our cigarettes and admiring the stars, clear and large in the huge sky, June told me about Jesus' love. "He loves you no matter what you've done or what you've said or who you've hurt or what thoughts you think. He simply loves you -- right now -- just as you are."

I thought, "He couldn't possibly love me. I'm not one of those nicey-nice girls who goes to church. I swear and smoke and drink. Nobody good loves a girl like that."

"He does love you," June insisted. She told me verses from the Bible that said He did. Verse after verse, she explained His love until finally I agreed that she might be right. The only reason I could begin to believe that Jesus loved me just the way I was, was because June had loved me the same way herself.

Later that night June asked, "Would you like to ask Jesus into your heart? Would you like to become a Christian tonight?"

I poked at the fire with a stick and lit another cigarette. My thoughts turned to the big event of my life I'd been planning for years, my high school graduation. It wasn't the kind of party a Christian would throw -- and I'd planned that party for a long time.

June was waiting for my answer, probably praying. As much as I wanted to please her, I wanted that party more. Across the camp fire I slowly shook my head no.

Chapter 7

June continued to love unconditionally, continued to listen and be my friend. To me she was the most special person I'd ever encountered. For brief moments I was glad I had left Linda's because if I hadn't, I wouldn't have met June.

Back at the Children's Home I spent the long summer days waiting for her letters. Mail came in the afternoon, and I always rushed to see if there was something for me. Even her handwriting on the envelope made me glad.

I took her letters to the rooftop where I could be alone. I slit the envelope open, trying to make the moment last. The pages were covered with things she wanted me to know about, particularly God's love for me and His goodness. Everything had a scripture number, proving, I guessed, that she hadn't made it up.

Sitting there I thought, "What if I hadn't planned that party?" But I had planned it and nothing was going to keep me from going through with it. I folded June's letter and put it back in the envelope and tucked it in my pocket. I would read it at least ten times before the next letter arrived.

"Does anyone want to go hear Billy Graham talk tonight?" It was the voice of the housemother, calling up the stairs to the girls' dorm. "Mr. Spencer from Calvary Temple is here and he's offered to bring anyone who wants to go, to the Billy Graham meeting."

"Who's Billy Graham?" I asked someone.

"Oh, he gives lectures on religion."

"Well, let's go; anything's better than sitting here. We can probably slip away and go bowling like we do on Sundays."

Six of us older girls, including Dottie, raced down the stairs and into the waiting car. When we arrived at the football stadium, it was obvious we weren't going to get away and go bowling. The crowd was so huge I knew we'd never find Mr. Spencer or our way back. Much to my disgust I ended up with the others on the 30-yard line at Memorial Stadium listening to some guy sing.

While Billy Graham talked, I thought about Rick, a boy who'd come by the Children's Home one evening while I was sitting outside on the grass. Rick had a gray convertible and it was easy to sneak out for a ride with him. Like every other boy I'd met, he had one thing on his mind. I needed the hugging and kissing and he said he needed the rest of what went with it. It was to me a good trade. I would probably invite him to my party.

Down on the field Billy Graham had finished his talk. The choir was singing the words, "Just as I am," and Billy Graham was asking people to come forward and make a decision for Christ. I answered him mentally.

"Someday, maybe, but not now."

"You may not get another chance," he announced on the public address system.

"What would my friends think?" I wondered.

"The only thing that matters is what the Lord thinks," he announced again.

"I'm having a graduation party."

"No matter what your plans are, a decision for Christ will make them better."

"No, I can't."

"Come now. Come down to the field."

"Not yet."

"Don't put your decision off another day."

"I'm not good enough."

"Don't wait until you're good enough."

On and on I objected, and each time Billy Graham announced the answer to my objection. Suddenly I was crying! Not out loud, I was too tough for that, but inside of me I was sobbing. I looked towards the aisles, wanting to go down, but I'd have to walk past Dottie, Jean, Sandy and Orin -- all the girls who looked up to me. On my other side was my friend Judy. I whispered, "If I go down, will you go with me?" Immediately I was sorry I'd asked, for I could see she was shocked. Her eyes said, "You, Fran, you of all people?" Then Billy Graham said, "If anyone around you looks like they want to come, tap them on the shoulder."

The man behind me tapped my shoulder. Suddenly, I was standing. Then I was walking down the stairs to the field. I had the same thick crust wrapped around my heart that I'd had at the train depot in Montana, but the words the choir kept singing were somehow tearing away that crust. "*Just as I am.* Me, Fran, so messed up, so scared, so lonely, so hurting, *just as I am.*" Even with these thoughts, embarrassment flooded me. What would the others think? I was the cool one who didn't play games, sing silly songs, or get hassled. I glanced sideways to see if my friends were smirking. To my surprise, Judy, Dottie, Sandy, Jean and Orin were walking behind me, down onto the field, across the 30-yard line, making a decision for Jesus.

A counselor met me. She gave me a yellow card with the day of my commitment on it. I looked at her in disbelief, resenting her. This was between me and God. Why wouldn't she go away? Something right and important was happening in my life that I couldn't comprehend, and I wanted to be alone.

"Where do you live?" The counselor's voice intruded. "What is your address?" I reluctantly gave her the information. Finally she left, and I stood there fingering the yellow commitment card. What kind of a decision had I actually made? I looked at the card. It said I'd made a decision for Christ, that I'd become a Christian.

The next day I quickly wrote a letter to June sharing the evening's events, while at the same time trying to be the old, cool me. "Dear June, guess what? Well, last night at the Billy Graham meeting I became a Christian. I guess this means I'm going to have to give up sinning. I hope this doesn't mean life's going to be a drag. Anyway, I knew you'd want to know."

Afterwards when I thought about it, it seemed strange, but from that point on I almost instinctively knew that some of the things I'd been doing were wrong. The big wrong was stealing. Now no one had told me that stealing was not right, but I somehow knew it wasn't. When I gave up stealing, I automatically gave up alcohol. All the beer and wine I drank was stolen from stores or other people.

And I sensed, too, that I should give up cigarettes. In fact, I gave up cigarettes many times, but always went back to them. It wasn't just the nicotine in my bloodstream, it was the whole ritual -- finding a place alone, especially when I was angry or hurt about something -- lighting up, inhaling, blowing out the first puff of smoke -- it gave me a sense of security of all being right with the world for a few minutes.

As far as boys went, what was there to give up? Sure, Rick had one thing he wanted, but somehow I never thought of it as sin. Sex was something no one outside of the guys I dated ever talked about. As far as I was concerned, it was part of the package of dating. If dating was acceptable, so was sex.

In a few days I received some literature from the Billy Graham people. I read every word and I began to understand a little that Jesus had died for me and taken my sins away. For the first time I was glad for the counselor who had taken my address.

In a few days a letter from June was waiting for me. I tucked it in my pocket and climbed the stairs to my favorite spot by the roof. Getting ready for the treat of June's letter, I lit a cigarette, inhaled deeply and blew the smoke out slowly. Then I ripped the envelope open. She was happy for me, but a little sad for herself that she hadn't been there when I made my decision for the Lord. She urged me to begin reading the Bible.

I sat there reading her words over and over, thinking about her advice. I'd already tried to read the little King James' Bible I'd carried from foster home to foster home through the years. It didn't make any sense. I'd decided a long time ago that Bible reading must be only for old people or at least for people who had been Christians for years. Now here was June saying to read the Bible.

Shortly after that, in my room, I had just settled back on my pillow when in the corner of the room I saw a strange light. It hadn't slowly filtered in like the moonlight does. No, it was suddenly there where there had been no light before. It wasn't from the street, for it was far brighter. I felt drawn to it, for in that light or maybe He was the light, which ever it was, Jesus was there in my room. He looked at me with a great and wonderful love. Then as quickly as He'd come, he faded from my sight. But in those few moments something had happened to me. From then on, I had an insatiable desire to read the Bible.

The next day I headed straight for the Home's library. There, tucked on the back shelf I found a thick book, *The Children's Book of Bible Stories*. I checked it out and carried it reverently down to my room. That night I began to read. Soon I was so fascinated that I was reading under the covers with a flashlight at night, reading and making notes, reading and smoking. I read through the children's book and then returned to the King James' version. This time it made sense. I was determined to read it all. I even made a list of every king from Saul to Zedekiah, and tried to memorize their names.

It was from that point on that one of the strangest

things to date happened. For no reason that I could think of, Rick quit picking me up. I sat out on the lawn as I'd done many times before and waited. No gray convertible turned the corner. No one called, "Hey, Fran, do you want a ride?" I couldn't believe it -- jilted for the first time. "Well," I easily consoled myself, "there are plenty of other boys." But even though I waited in the same spot where the guys had always stopped before, not a single boy came by the rest of the summer. Eagerly, I awaited the start of my senior year. For sure I would meet a few boys. But again not one noticed me. It was as if they were looking through me, somehow not seeing me. The deep red of fall passed and the cold and rain of winter came and finally gave way to the budding green of spring. Still I had not had one date. I never thought of it as God's protection, that I needed time to learn how to live His ways, time to break off old habit patterns. I just thought of it as peculiar and strange.

Meanwhile, there was something important I had to take care of. Soon after I became a Christian, it began to occur to me that I couldn't blame Linda for what had happened at her house. I lay in bed and mulled the Montana events over and over in my mind. Yes, I had disobeyed. Yes, Linda did have to put Lee first. As I finally went to sleep, it was with the alarming realization that Linda had done her best, and perhaps I was the one who might just possibly have been wrong.

In the morning I woke up to the fresh sunlight warming the floor. Somewhere close, I could hear the "cheep, cheep" of a family of late summer robins. I reached for a piece of notebook paper and a pencil. "Dear Linda, Just thought you would like to know what's been going on in my life since I last saw you at the train depot . . ." Even though the words weren't exactly, "I'm sorry, forgive me," that was what I meant. I hoped Linda would understand.

A week later Dottie and I were together on the third floor. "You have a visitor in the parlor," one of the workers told us.

Our eyes met. "Linda!" The only person who would possibly visit us was Linda. Fred was still far away in the navy. Although I'd never lost the longing to see Mother, I knew it wouldn't be her after all these years. No, it had to be Linda. All the way down those two flights of cement stairs to the visitor's parlor, my heart pounded with fear because I wanted everything to be right between us. The parlor door was open, but Dottie and I hung in the doorway, afraid to go in. There was Linda, and not only Linda, but Lee and little Randy and her new baby, Sheila. "Hello," I said cautiously.

"Hello, Fran. Hello, Dottie."

Dottie's hello was followed by an awkward silence. Finally, little Randy broke the tension. "I can do a somersault," he said. He jumped off a wicker chair and went to the middle of the room. His somersault, a half sprawl, was so comical I laughed. Dottie laughed, and then Linda and Lee laughed. The ice was broken and suddenly we were all talking at once. "Let's get out of this stuffy place," Linda said. "Let's go somewhere and get a milk shake."

I nodded, "Sure." Inside me I was crying with happiness. Everything was all right between Linda and me again.

The day after Linda left, I began my senior year. Dottie, who was beginning the tenth grade, and I walked together to Roosevelt High School. It wasn't long before I had the situation sized up. There was the wild crowd and there was the crowd that lived within the rules. For a few weeks I stood on the edge, deciding which direction I should take. Dottie and I talked about it on our walks to school. "Who are you going to hang around with this year?" I asked her.

"I'm not sure. What about you?"

"I don't know either. I know I'd fit in with the wild kids. I'm just not sure about the others, but they seem okay." I went back and forth in my mind. Both groups were appealing. One, because I was so familiar with it; the other, because I felt an almost unexplainable pull towards it.

Finally one morning as we kicked our way through crisp mounds of brown autumn leaves, I told Dottie I'd made my decision. "I'm not going to get mixed up with the wild kids. I think I'm supposed to stay away from people that would get me in trouble."

Dottie laughed, "And that wouldn't take very much, would it?" Quickly she was serious. "Well, if that's the way you're going to do it, Fran, then that's the way I'll do it too."

In October Dottie and I were summoned once more to the visitor's parlor. There sitting on one of the straight-backed wicker chairs was Miss Blackstone, and she was smiling. "Fran, Dottie, I have good news." And she did. Outside of the one fact that I continually longed to hear that Mother had somehow contacted the welfare office, her news was great. A foster home had been found for both of us. Hurrah! We could leave the Children's Home. Maybe, just maybe, this would be the kind of home we'd always wanted.

We packed our meager supply of belongings and climbed into Miss Blackstone's car. She smiled, "Fran, you seem different to me. I'm pleased to see you looking so happy."

"I'm doing fine," I answered her easily. As we put the suitcases in the trunk of her car, we talked together almost like friends.

Miss Blackstone has changed, I thought. At the time I didn't think that maybe I was the one who had changed instead. In the car Dottie, Miss Blackstone and I were all quiet. Perhaps Dottie, too, was lost in memories. I could still picture myself, a raggedy four-year-old playing in the sandbox while my mother was given artificial respiration by the firemen. I could see in my mind's eye the ride in the police car, the Children's Home, a succession of foster homes, the home where maggots squirmed on the window sill, scoldings and loneliness, wet beds, Mr. Schmidt making fun of me, the hired man, Linda's, detention. Now we were heading for our thirteenth foster home. "Dear God," I prayed, "please make it a good home."

Peggy and Jim Shriver were in their early 30's and had two young children of their own. Their home was ordinary, but it was a house we wouldn't have to feel ashamed of. Jim was a golfer and except for stories, we'd never known anyone who'd golfed before. Peggy, besides being young, was pretty. We didn't have to be ashamed of her as our foster mother as we'd been so many times before. To us, being with the Shrivers was high class living like we'd never seen before.

They even wanted us to call them Mom and Dad. This was the one thing I couldn't do. I don't know whether it was the deep hurt of always wanting my own mother or the painful succession of Moms who'd only lasted a short while. Whatever, the only cloud was not being able to call these good people anything except, "Hey."

The neighbor across the street was a minister and he invited us to his church. Peggy and Jim went occasionally, but I went every chance I could get. Since it was a liberal church and talked more of social issues than the Bible, I found myself more and more listening to the Christian radio broadcasts. In the back of our clothes closet was a small window and I leaned out the window so the smell of my cigarettes wouldn't be discovered, while I listened to the "The Bible Hour," "Back to the Bible," and the astounding meetings of an evangelist named Brother Ralph. While others made fun of his words, I found him feeding me, teaching me, helping me to know so many things that no one else had ever thought to tell me.

By now I'd somehow got the message that smoking was "out" for Christians. It was a somewhat confused message. I'd learned that Jesus had died for my sins and made heaven available to me no matter what I did. I couldn't earn it because it was a free gift. On the other hand I was hearing from some of my radio preachers that I'd better quit smoking or... The words weren't exact, but the impression was that I'd never get to heaven if I smoked. I was caught in the middle of my own physical needs. I needed cigarettes, I craved them, Christian or not.

One Sunday afternoon after hearing on the radio how you must courageously step out and quit smoking, I decided once and for all I'd quit for good. I dropped my last pack of cigarettes in the garbage can behind the house. I was through, through forever, with smoking. After dinner I cleaned the kitchen and went upstairs, tired and ready for bed. And there on the bed was a stack of books for school, my homework! I'd forgotten about it. Now I had to stay up and do it when all I wanted to do was crawl into bed. I opened the history book and began reading.

Almost without realizing what I was doing, I grabbed the flashlight and headed downstairs for the garbage can. I found the cigarettes right where I'd thrown them. As soon as I got to my room, I closed the door and lit up. If that teacher was going to force a lot of work on me, it was her fault I needed a cigarette to get through it.

The highlight of those days living with the Shrivers happened almost routinely. I came home from school and found no one at home. I hung up my coat and put my books in my room. There on the bed that Dottie and I shared was a note pinned to the pillow. I picked it up and began to read:

Dear Dot and Fran,

Sometimes it's easier to write what you feel than it is to say it.

You girls have brought daddy and me nothing but joy and happiness -- *I love you*, in the three short months more than you'd ever dream. This is your home the same as Jack's and Jill's -- Fran we'll manage somehow to keep you in school -- if we are in Seattle. Dot you break my heart when you are sad -- so if something is bothering my littlest big girl -- I want to know. That's what Mothers are for. To lend a big understanding ear. I'm proud to call you both my daughters. I feel cheated that you are not really mine.

By the time you get this I will be slaving over a hot golf course -- Keep your fingers crossed for me, my little cherubs.

Love, Mother

I continued to stand in the middle of the floor, holding the letter, once more crying inside. No one knows the loneliness of the rowdiest girl in detention or the wildest girl at a party. No one knows that she probably never had a letter signed, "Love, Mother," and that maybe that's why she's rowdy or wild. There in that minute or two something happened inside me, for somehow I understood that the part of me which had always wanted to be recognized and accepted had been calmed. I knew it hadn't gone away because I still wanted acceptance, but the insatiable need for love that I'd carried with me since before I could remember had, in a moment with that letter, been somehow diffused.

Later, Dottie read the letter and graciously let me be the one to have it. I carried it in my wallet so that when I needed it, I could take it out and reread it, lingering over the words, "Love, Mother."

Graduation!

The big night finally arrived, but not with the fanfare I'd once anticipated. Peggy and Jim Shriver along with Dottie were in the audience as I walked across the stage and received my diploma. Afterwards, a group of girls from school got together for a slumber party at a home in the country. I laid my sleeping bag in the field a little apart from the others. Off in the distance I saw the lights of Seattle. Above me were the stars, standing out clear enough to count. For a moment I sighed for the party that was to have been on this night. Putting my hands behind my head, I leaned back and reflected on the peace that had come into my life in the past year. Simple peace. Quiet peace. God's peace. Was that the way it was always going to be? Or could there be more turbulence ahead?

Chapter 8

I decided on Seattle Pacific College, a Christian college, even though the State would have paid my way to the University of Washington. I wanted to be around other Christians, although it meant working to pay my way through. It was worth it for many reasons.

One reason was the friendship I'd developed with Christian men. During the previous years of attending church and listening to Christian radio stations, I'd come to understand God's plan for the relationship between the sexes. Yes, He'd created the sex act that so many of my dates had ended with, but He'd made it for a different reason than what I'd been led to believe. Once I'd thought sex was "just the way it was." Now I learned that it was a holy act to be shared, not just between any two people, but between husband and wife.

It was a realization that didn't hit me between the eyes, but one that came slowly. Sex was one of God's ways of uniting husbands and wives and making their love and relationship special outside of all other relationships. Somehow I came to understand it was a love act more than it was a sex act and that a child which came

Fran's Mother and Father

I
LIFE AT THE SCHMIDT'S

1. Fourteen-year old Fran and her sister, Dottie, on the farm.

2. Dottie, Mrs Schmidt and Fran on a visit to Victoria, B.C.

3. Fran and "Tiny."

4. Fran and Dottie "clowning it up" at the Puyallup Fair.

II
IN MONTANA WITH LINDA

1. Sweet Sixteen!

2. Fifteen-year old Fran as a high school sophomore.

3. Fran on the left as a member of the "in" group.

4. Fran hunting in Montana.

5. Fran leaving Montana for the Youth Center in 1951.

III
BACK IN SEATTLE

1. Fran with a cook at the Children's Home.

2. Cabin "G" at the Salvation Army Camp, Lake Boren.

3. Fran's confidant, June, Cabin G's counselor.

4. At Calvary Temple in Seattle where she received her initial teaching after accepting Jesus.

IV
COLLEGE DAYS

1.&2. Fran during her Practice Teaching stint at Ronald Grade School in Seattle.

3. Celebrating "Homecoming."

4. Fran and her roommate "clown" for the photographer.

5. Fran and Russ at her graduation from Seattle Pacific College in 1956.

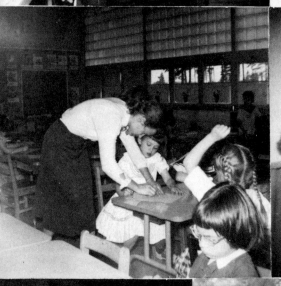

V
MARRIAGE AND FAMILY

1. Fran and Russ on their wedding day, December 21, 1955 (Photo Credit: Sydney M. Merrihew).

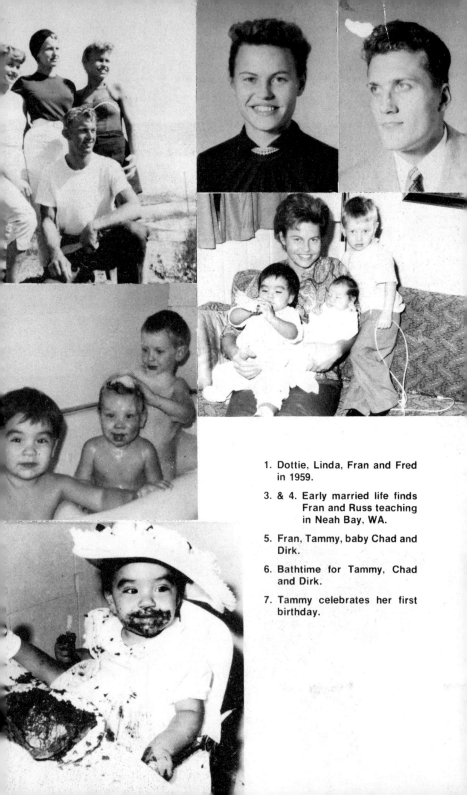

1. Dottie, Linda, Fran and Fred in 1959.

3. & 4. Early married life finds Fran and Russ teaching in Neah Bay, WA.

5. Fran, Tammy, baby Chad and Dirk.

6. Bathtime for Tammy, Chad and Dirk.

7. Tammy celebrates her first birthday.

8. Fran, Linda and Dottie.

9. Tracy blesses the Lance household - Fran, Russ, baby Tracy, Chad, Dirk and Tammy.

10. All ready to go to the adoption agency to pick up Rusty - Tracy, Chad, Tammy and Dirk.

11. Love grows for Russ and Fran . . .

12. . . . And so does the family -- Fran and baby Rusty.

13. Fran and Rusty on the cover of the AGLOW Magazine, Winter 1976.

14. Back to the bath -- Tracy, Tammy, Chad, Dirk, and Rusty.

15. The complete Lance family, 1971 -- Russ, Fran, Chad, Tammy, Rusty, Tracy and Dirk.

16. The Lance family continues to grow in years, 1978 -- Chad, Fran, Russ, Tammy, Dirk, Rusty and Tracy.

17. Fran with her sister, Linda, who serves as Vice-President of Retreats on the Eastern Montana Area board.

VI
FRAN'S REUNION WITH HER REAL FAMILY

1. Fran and her newly found relatives in 1978.

VII
FRAN'S MINISTRY

1. & 2. Fran shares at an Aglow meeting.

3. Fran at her desk in the International office.

from this was something beautiful and not just something to fear as I'd once thought.

With this new frame of mind firmly established, I found that boys began to be interested in me again. My first college date was with a boy named Ron. We went bowling and stopped for a hamburger on the way back to the campus. He saw me to my door, no kiss, no touching of any type on his part. No subtle seduction on my part. I had once loved seeing how long it took to get a guy aroused; now I wanted to see how long we could go without holding hands.

I confided all these thing to Dottie who was married by now. She had come to the college campus to let me see her new baby son, Danny, and I was showing her around. "I'm really happy," I told her. "I like the feeling I have after a date. I'd give anything if some of those things in the past hadn't happened."

"But they did," she said. "Once they've happened, they've happened."

"But I've asked God to forgive me."

"Did He?"

Even though Dottie had gone forward at the Billy Graham revival, she hadn't been affected in the same way I was. She knew she was a Christian, but she didn't enjoy the Bible or the Christian radio like I did. Maybe it was because she was younger or maybe it was because I had more pain to be freed of. I answered her as best I could, "Yes, when Jesus died, He took away all the punishment for my sins. When I asked Him to forgive me, He did. Every sin I've ever committed in my whole life has been forgiven and my life has started all over."

Dottie looked with hope. "I wish my sins were forgiven."

I was determined there would be no more sexual sin in my life. I knew I wanted to be pure because Jesus loved me and had forgiven me so much. I wanted it for Him as well as for myself. I needed acceptance, I still could feel it in me, but I knew that I had to find it another way. Being pure was almost too easy that first year on campus, and then I met Philip.

We dated several times, casually as I had learned to make my dates. Soon it was May. The first term was almost over. Philip would be leaving for Alaska for four months. Even though he was not a special boy friend, I suddenly realized I would miss him. On our last date we ended up parked on a dead-end street with a beautiful view of the Seattle harbor.

"Four months is a long time," he said.

"I know, I'll miss you."

He kissed me good-bye, a long, warm kiss that said he was sorry we'd be separated. He kissed me again and again. I should have stopped him right there. I could feel his body growing eager and the restlessness of his hands. We kissed longingly. It was a warm spring night and four months seemed forever.

Compared to my dates before I was a Christian, we'd done nothing, but as a Christian I knew we were going too far. There was no excuse now. I knew better. I knew he was aroused and I knew I was responsible, simply because I hadn't said no.

"Please, Fran, one more kiss."

I wanted that kiss. I'd always loved kissing and hugging. I loved the tension in his body . . . but I knew we couldn't stay there any longer and not get into serious trouble. "No Philip, we have to go."

Back in my room I was desolate. "Fran, that was sin. You've sinned. You knew better. You shouldn't have returned those kisses. Jesus forgave all your past sins and now you've ruined everything."

All day long I went over the guilt of that experience, telling myself how I'd failed. By evening time it occurred to me what to do, something I should have done immediately. Down on my knees in my room, I prayed, "Jesus, please forgive me again. I'm sorry. I want in my heart to turn from this kind of sin forever." In that moment of seeking forgiveness, the weight of guilt slipped from my shoulders. How could I accuse myself when the Lord Jesus had already forgiven me?

Although I later wrote Philip a letter asking his forgiveness, the whole episode never brought any guilt again, and soon became nothing more than another forgiven shadow of the past.

One morning during the first year of college, I woke up and turned over. "Oh, dear God, no." I was wet, soaking wet. I lay there feeling all the shame of the little girl in the Children's Home. I heard the scoldings and the accusations of carelessness echoing through the years. I'd thought I was through with wetting. At Linda's I hadn't been wet too much and at the Shrivers hardly at all. Wasn't it ever going to stop? I got up and pulled the sheets off the bed and pulled off my pajamas. As I stepped in the shower, I was angry, not at myself really, just angry at anyone who could think that little kids or big kids would ever wet the bed deliberately. What I had no way of knowing then, was that at last I'd outgrown it. That morning, that freshman year in college, was the last time I ever woke up wet again.

"Well, Fran, if you really want to find your mother, why don't you look her up through the Bureau of Missing Persons." I had confided in Loretta, a waitress I worked with, about my mother and the desire that wouldn't leave me to see her again. She was emphatic with her advice. "My husband works for the Bureau of Missing Persons. Why don't you let him help you? If your mother was ever arrested, they'll have a picture of her and you can go from there."

I was nervous as I climbed the steps of the police station. Police were people I just naturally shied away from, from force of habit, I guess. Yet that day they were very helpful and before long I found myself looking through one yellowed "mug" book after another. I looked carefully at each face before I looked at the name because I was so sure I'd recognize her. After a couple of hours I came across a picture that almost made my heart stop. The name was Fred Hall. It was my father's name. Could this balding man with a number across his chest possibly be my own Dad? I was overjoyed beyond words. I'd always wondered what my father looked like. Many times I'd envisioned him in my mind, but, of course, it was only a game I'd played. If Mama had had a picture of him, I'd never seen it.

It was verified that this man was indeed my father. I was allowed to have a copy of his picture. Right away I took it to an artist. "Just give him a little hair, " I said "and could you you put a shirt and tie on him instead of those numbers?" When the artist was finished, he looked just like a real father should look. The copies I had made were the biggest surprise Linda, Dottie and Fred had ever received.

Meanwhile, I went back to continue my search for my mother. The next day I found her. She had been arrested and charged with being "a sailor's girl," a term used in those days for a prostitute. I was given her latest address and set out to find her. With a pounding heart I climbed up the steps of a ramshackle house. A scruffy looking man answered my timid knock. I showed him Mama's name and asked if he knew where she was. He was just about to say no when he remembered that he'd received a letter from her asking for her things. He searched around for a long time before he found it. At last he brought it out to me. "I don't know if she's still there. It was some time ago," he said.

That night I sat down and wrote my mother a letter.

"Dear mother, I got your address from a man who used to know you. I thought maybe I could come to see you for Christmas. I'm a sophomore in college now and I work in a restaurant, but I'm sure I could get some time off to come. Will you let me know if it's all right with you. Love, your daughter, Fran.

P.S. Linda, Fred and Dottie are all fine."

Every day I waited for an answer. A month later it came. A letter from my mother! I ran my hand over the envelope and looked at her handwriting. My very own mother had addressed it to me, her daughter. I was 19 and trying to be grown up, but the lump in my throat wouldn't go away. It was a long letter and she ended it by saying . . . "Let me know when you're coming and I'll meet you at the station. Love, Mother."

Joyfully, I went shopping. Although it took almost all the money I'd saved for the next semester, I bought a beautiful, blue coat with fur trim on the collar. I just couldn't meet her in my old coat when I had such a burning desire to make her proud of me. I sent her a quick note telling her when I'd arrive and I added, "Look for a girl in a blue coat with a fur trim."

A few days before Christmas I boarded a train heading for Chicago. I was as excited as a child and as scared as I'd ever been in my whole life. At the cavernous Chicago depot I searched the faces of every woman, wondering which one was my mother. Then I saw her, looking as she should look -- tall and loving. She was looking around as if she were trying to locate someone.

I wanted to give her time to recognize me so I walked up and down in front of her, hoping she would notice me. When she didn't say anything, I finally managed the courage to ask, "Are you looking for someone?"

She smiled. Before I could tell her I was the one she was looking for, she answered, "I'm looking for my son."

I walked away embarrassed and disappointed and continued to look and wait. All of a sudden I was seven years old again, standing on the corner looking for the foster mother who never came.

At last I heard my name on the loud speaker. Then I was on the phone talking to her. She explained she had no shoes and couldn't come to meet me. "That's okay, Mother. It really is," I assured her. "I'll be there as soon as I can."

The cab turned onto the littered Skid Road street, and stopped in front of a condemned hotel. I could hear the boarded hotel windows shake in the wind that blew from Lake Michigan. I wrapped the blue coat tightly around me and, shivering, pulled open the sagging front door. Old papers were strewn in the hall, dirt was everywhere, covering the floor and stairs. I walked to the back of the hotel and turned into a dimly lit hall. My footsteps echoed and I realized that Mother was the only one living there. Finally, I found her room number and knocked. I could hear the shuffle of footsteps coming to the door. The door opened slowly and there she was.

I had remembered her being so tall, but now to my surprise we were just about the same height. She looked at me with confused uncertainty, and I realized she had expected me to be that little child she'd left behind. Instead, here I was a woman. It seemed an eternity that we stood looking at each other. Finally I reached out to her and wrapped her in my arms. Then her arms went around me and she patted my head over and over as she'd done when I was four years old.

The hotel room held a bed with grimy sheets, a lopsided table and two rickety chairs. There was an equally grimy bathroom off to the side. "Let me get you some coffee," she said. We sat at the lop-sided table and she poured my coffee into a cracked green mug. It was a moment I'd eagerly anticipated—yet, it was all so different than I'd planned.

In the end, confusion triumphed over all the years. Mother talked about the weather. "Yes, it's really cold here in Chicago." I waited for her to ask about what I'd done for the past 15 years, but she didn't ask. Didn't she want to know how I'd made out without her? Instead, she rambled more about the cold. "Yes, it's really winter now." I waited for her to ask about Linda, Fred and Dottie. Two hours went by and Mother switched from coffee to wine. I figured I'd better tell her abut myself without waiting for her to ask. I told her about the Billy Graham meeting and how I'd gone forward and that I was a Christian. She said she thought it was nice but I could see she didn't understand. I tried to tell her about the others. "Mother, Linda has two babies and her husband is a good provider. Fred's in the Navy and Dorothy (Mother had never known about her name being changed to Dottie) has a new little son.

Mother shook her head as if she were trying to comprehend it all and poured herself more wine. The wind shook the old hotel and it rattled. Out in the hall I could hear footsteps which slowed down outside the door. Mother was growing drunk and with each hour I was growing more afraid. I drank coffee and stayed awake because I was too frightened to sleep. Mother drank more wine. By the morning of Christmas Eve, she had no idea who I was or what I was doing there. When she passed out on the grimy bed I slipped out the door. I realized it had almost been a miracle that she'd been sober when I arrived.

At the depot I caught the train for Seattle. I kept gazing out the window, seeing and yet not seeing the Christmas decorations and lights throughout the countryside.

Inside I was suffering in a way I'd never suffered before.

I knew there was only one process in the world that could take away that hurt. "I forgive her, Jesus. I forgive her for leaving us when we were little, for not coming to see us, for not writing. I forgive her for being an alcoholic and for the way she lives. I forgive her, Jesus. I forgive her. I forgive her for not asking about my life, for not asking about the others. I forgive her for getting drunk . . ." Slowly, as I forgave, the Lord showed me something I hadn't understood before. Mother couldn't come and see us because she couldn't handle the guilt. She couldn't ask about the last 15 years because the guilt of her leaving us was too great, and the guilt that kept her from asking about the others was the guilt that was keeping her an alcoholic.

"Jesus, I do forgive her. I hold nothing against her. Please bless her. Heal her and bring her to know You as her Savior."

The train rolled on through the Rocky Mountains, across the Columbia River and on towards home. With each mile closer to Seattle the hurts of the years, especially of the past two days, diminished as if they were buried somewhere along the way by the prayer of forgiveness.

Chapter
9

"Y̵ou've got to see this new guy on campus, Fran. He's dreamy," Esther, my roommate announced. I didn't want to be bothered; I was too busy to go looking at some guy my roommate had already picked for herself.

"Did you see him? Did you see Russ?" she asked again.

"Not yet."

"Fran, have you seen Russ yet?"

"No."

The next day just to silence her I went over to the gym and peeked through the door. Russ was out on the floor shooting baskets and I had to admit I liked what I saw. He was over six feet with a strong, husky build and a crew cut, the all-American type of guy. "Not bad," I told myself, "not at all." But, of course, Russ belonged to my roommate even though he had no idea he was spoken for.

Russ and Esther dated some, but as it turned out, Russ wasn't ready to be claimed by anyone. First of all, he came from a family of ten brothers and sisters and he enjoyed going home on the weekends and being with them. Also, he didn't have the money for dates. What he did have, though, was a big Hudson and a big heart, big enough to take lots of us girls bowling or to the movies. By now Esther had someone else she was interested in, and I decided it was time Russ noticed me for myself, instead of thinking of me as just one of the girls he toted around. One evening when he was dropping us back at the dorm, I slipped the keys out of the ignition of his car and took them to my room.

Then I dashed upstairs and watched him empty his pockets for the third time and check the sidewalk and peer into the street. Finally I leaned out the window, dangling the keys. "Are you looking for these? You left them in the ignition. Don't you know someone could have stolen them?"

He looked up and sputtered something. But he smiled, too.

"Here, catch." I tossed his keys and he caught them one-handed. But my plan worked. A couple of days later he came by the restaurant where I worked and asked me if I wanted to see *The Glen Miller Story*.

Since my experience with Philip, I was cautious with the guys I dated so that nothing would get started between us that was wrong in the sight of God. With Russ I didn't even have to work at it. His standards were far higher than mine. Over a coke he explained where he stood. "The responsibility for conduct on a date belongs to the boy," he told me. "Holding hands shouldn't be taken lightly and kissing a girl should only be on a special occasion. I sipped my coke and looked across the table at this handsome guy, hardly believing my ears.

"You're a really special guy, Russ," I told him. "Tell me what makes you think like that."

He told me that when he'd been 12 years old, he'd felt the hand of the Lord on his life and had experienced a touch by God. "I knew from then I was to be His servant," he confided, "that somehow in my life I would be serving Him." I went back to the dorm that night, amazed at this good-looking guy with a crew cut whose greatest goal was to serve the Lord.

We dated half a dozen times during my sophomore year and then the year was almost over. He drove his Hudson up to the curb beside my door so we could talk a while before I went in.

"Fran," he asked, "can I kiss you?"

I was so surprised I didn't know what to do. No one had actually asked before. I shook my head yes and he reached across the car and gave me a stiff, funny little half kiss that sort of slipped away. Then he kissed me again, quite satisfactorily. One real kiss, that was all.

And I was in love. I'd never met anyone quite like him before. His life had been kept as clean as mine had been sullied. He loved the Lord. He wanted to serve Him. He was handsome, tall, quiet. I knew he would be loyal. At the end of May he asked me to marry him. I looked into those blue eyes and pictured a dozen babies all looking just like him. I was loved, I was accepted. I put my head against his chest and felt his arms around me. "Yes, Russ, I want more than anything else in the world to be your wife." I accepted gladly.

With a guy like Russ I knew I could give up smoking easily. I tossed my cigarettes in the waste basket and covered them with a wad of notebook paper. It was good to be through smoking at last.

When I accepted his proposal, I knew I should confess my past. Also, I knew I might lose him if I did. "Lord, help me to accept whatever happens when I tell him." Then I prayed for the right time and the right words. The right time came one evening when Russ and I were sitting in the Hudson outside my rooming house. "Russ, I want you to know about what happened to me when I was a little girl." I told him about the hired man.

He just sat there and looked at me, not quite comprehending. I was sure he understood my innocence, but I knew he needed time to adjust. He walked me to the door in silence. The following days he didn't mention it again.

But there was more to be honest about than just the

hired man. I waited awhile and then one night I asked, "Russ, do you want to walk around the campus for awhile?" The Seattle Pacific College campus is built on the side of a steep hill so any kind of a walk around eventually meant hiking up a hill. That night we climbed two steep blocks and stopped to catch our breath and look out at the north end of Seattle. I knew it was time to tell him and I was so afraid my stomach hurt and my heart hammered like a storm at sea against my chest. "Russ, I want to tell you a little more about myself." He didn't answer, so I plunged in. I sketched a picture that must have been hard for him to accept. When I was done, he still didn't answer.

Silence. A plane went overhead. Cars whizzed by in the distance. I waited and still he said nothing.

Many years later I found out how hurt and angry he'd been. He'd wanted to be first in my life. He had worried how my past would affect our children. In a husky voice, he'd finally broken the silence by saying, "Come on. Let's go back."

I reached for his hand and held it in both of mine. "I'm sorry, Russ. I'd give anything if it hadn't happened."

There was still silence as we walked back to the dorm. "I'll see you tomorrow," he said. And he didn't kiss me good night.

There was another girl in the rooming house who smoked. "I need a cigarette," I told her. I lit one slowly, thinking about Russ and about his reactions. A thousand thoughts raced across my mind. "Dear God, why did that all have to happen? Dear God, why is he so silent?" I lit another one. "Why, why, why?"

Russ went home and prayed about it and whatever pain he experienced was between the Lord and himself. We never discussed my past again. But that summer Russ had plans to spend time on the East Coast; instead he stayed in Seattle. I never knew if he wanted to be with me or if it was because he didn't trust me enough to leave me on my own.

Even so, happy times followed. My senior and his

post-graduate year were times of contentment. After his graduation, Russ took a year of study to become a teacher while I finished my senior year. The wedding was set for December. We found a little trailer that needed fixing up and would be just perfect for the final six months of school.

Two days before the wedding we spent all day and evening working in the trailer, cleaning, painting, and stopping just long enough for a peanut butter sandwich. When we opened the door to go, we found that nearly a foot of snow had fallen and we hadn't even known it. There was no way Russ could get his car started and there was nothing to do but spend the night together.

By this time, so close to the wedding, Russ had allowed us the privilege of some hugging and kissing. We sat together on the side of the bed in the tiny trailer. Russ put his arm around me. In a short while I felt an urgency to his kisses that he'd always guarded before.

"Fran," he whispered.

"What, Russ?" He didn't answer, but I knew he was thinking, "I will, if you will."

A thousand emotions it seemed went through me. I was in love with this man. I felt in my own body that I wanted his love. He was the strong one. If he said it was okay, then it probably was. Yet, I knew, deep down, I knew, that engaged or not, in love or not, that this was sin. God had given us rules for our own good. He meant for us to keep them. Somehow I also knew that this was a test. It didn't matter that Russ was young and virile. It was that very fact that made the test so real. And it was a test that God allowed. Despite the warm feeling of his arms wrapped around me and the sweetness of his kisses, the words I had to say were not as hard as I thought they would be. "No, Russ, we have to wait."

The moment was over. The test was passed.

Some time went by before I understood a little of what the test had been about. If we'd sinned, God would have forgiven us and we would have started all over again, that was true. But would Russ ever have totally trusted me?

On the other hand, passing the test brought a blessing that overwhelmed me as I considered it in the days ahead. My confession of the past had deeply alarmed Russ. Now he would always know that the past was over, that I could be trusted and that he would never have to doubt me. I sighed and breathed a silent prayer, "Thank you, Lord, for Russ, for our love, and for the difficulty of the test. Amen."

Chapter
10

"Russ, what are we doing wrong? Why aren't kids who become Christians living Christian lives?"

"I wish I knew," he replied.

We were in a small apartment in Alaska where we had been serving a mission board and teaching for two years.

"I'm sure it's our fault. If only we could reach them, Russ. What should we be doing differently?"

He admitted he had no idea. We had many conversations like this where we blamed ourselves, trying to find a reason for the things that were going wrong in our lives. It was a discouraging time, working with young people, helping them to become Christians and then standing powerless while they slipped away.

"Do you ever feel there is more to the Christian life than what we're experiencing?" I asked him.

"Sometimes I do," he admitted, "but I don't know what it is."

That was as far as our conversation ever went. If there was more to life, we hadn't heard what it was. It had been eight years since our wedding, since the time we had dreamed of serving the Lord together, and in that time we had spent two years teaching on an Indian reservation at Neah Bay, Washington, one summer traveling in Europe and three years going between New York and California, so that Russ could get his Master's Degree from Biblical Seminary in New York. Now here we were in Alaska, completing two years of missionary work. I remembered how wonderful our future of serving the Lord together had seemed, and now...now I wasn't so sure. However, the discouragement about Christian work wasn't the only thing eating at me. In fact, it may have been just a symptom of my real problem. I wanted a baby. So far there had been none.

Three years before, a medical consultation following a series of tests had told us that there was only the slimmest possible chance of my getting pregnant. That slim chance had kept me going for the past three years and now I knew that there was not going to be a baby, no matter how badly I wanted one. So many times I'd prayed and there'd been so many disappointments. I looked across the room at Russ and tried to imagine what his child would be like. For a long time I sat there, pondering what I considered our greatest loss. Finally, he broke the silence that had fallen between us. "I promised to take some kids into town. Do you want to come along?"

"Thanks, anyway, but I think I'll stay here." The fact of the matter was that I wanted a cigarette. Whenever I was really down, I wanted one. As soon as Russ was gone, I ran to the store and bought a package of Lucky Strikes. For the past ten years I'd kept my smoking concealed, not only from Russ but from everyone. It just wouldn't do for a Christian missionary to smoke. Fortunately, in Alaska it was easy to find a place to be alone when I was worried or angry or disappointed. As much as I didn't want to smoke, I could always find a hiding spot and take those forbidden, but altogether satisfying, puffs.

When our contract in Alaska came to an end, Russ and I both knew we didn't want to stay any longer. He applied for a job in Seattle and was accepted as a teacher in a Christian school. The school also hired me as a substitute.

Even though all our questions about the power of Christianity continued unanswered, it was comforting to be in home territory. We'd even taken a tentative step towards getting a baby. We told Linda's doctor we'd like to adopt if one should ever come along. Of course, it was a long shot. There was no guarantee we'd get one, but it was a step.

During the school year, one month before our ninth anniversary, the phone rang one evening as Russ and I were sitting down to dinner.

"Fran, it's me, Linda. The doctor called. Your baby son is here."

"Russ," I screamed, "Russ, we've got a baby. There's a baby for us in Montana." Russ dropped his fork and came running. Excitedly, we talked to Linda, making arrangements. I'd leave for Montana the next day and bring our baby home the following day. Russ hung up the phone and held me in his arms. I put my head on his chest and let the tears come. We both knew that something special was happening in our lives and that from that day on we would never be the same again.

I stood in front of the nursery glass peering through the window at the newborn baby. I thought of the many, many heart-breaking times I'd stood with friends and relatives looking at someone else's baby. But this time was different. Behind the glass was our baby, Russ' and mine. My eyes skimmed the tiny bassinets, trying to find our little one. My baby. I hadn't realized babies looked so much alike. Then my eyes found the words, "Baby Lance," taped to the end of an empty bassinet. My heart started to pound as I looked around the nursery for the missing baby. I found him in the nurse's arms, face down, squealing as she burped him. Surely, she didn't have to treat him so roughly. Russ' and my baby! I could hardly tear my eyes away.

I motioned the nurse to bring him closer so I could see him. He really was beautiful. All I could do was silently thank God for this precious gift. Then I had to leave until the next day when I could hold him in my arms and take him home. As I left the hospital, my thoughts went towards the young mother who had given birth to Dirk, the name we had chosen to call him. I knew we would never meet, but knowing we were in the same hospital made me feel close to her. I wondered if perhaps by chance I could see her as I passed the open door of the Maternity Ward. Silently, I prayed a blessing on each mother as I quickly glanced from face to face on my way to the elevator. I felt a sadness as I thought of her leaving the hospital without the baby she had carried for nine months. But gratitude in my heart was intense as I left, both towards God and towards this young girl whom I would never know.

The next morning I signed the necessary papers in the lawyer's office and went to the hospital to pick up our four-day-old son. I gave the nurse the little blue outfit I'd brought from Seattle and watched with excitement as she dressed him. She tied on his too large hat, wrapped him in a blanket and handed him to me. The moment I had longed for had arrived.

My arms felt weak as I cuddled that little bundle close to me. He's ours, he's really ours. The nurse walked Linda and me to the door, opened it and waved goodbye. Walking through the bitter cold day in Montana, I climbed into the waiting car and drove off. "Lord, thank You. And, unknown mother, if you are still in the hospital, thank you, too."

At the airport Russ was waiting to meet us. He took his son in his arms and his eyes became misty. "Our baby," he said, putting one arm around me. The three of us, our family, walked through the airport together.

I thought of Mother. The ache in my heart for her had gone long ago. Yet there were moments like this when my thoughts turned to her. (After my visit to Chicago, we'd kept in touch by letter sporadically. I told her of Jesus' love and asked her to turn to Him and ask Him into her life. One surprising letter from her told me she had

94

married and moved to a different place. I could tell she was proud that she was married and it was as if she were saying, "Look, daughter, I've made good." Although she never answered me about receiving the Lord, I hoped her marriage was a sign of God's hand in her life. It wasn't too much later that I learned she had died.)

Once we were back home the first place Russ and I headed was to his mother's. She held her new grandson, letting his tiny hand grasp her wrinkled fingers.

Even though those were happy days for Russ and me, I was growing more and more aware of a need in my life for something more spiritually. I was happy, but not joyful. I was content, and yet discontent. "There has to be more," I whispered in prayer many times. Next door to me was another young mother who seemed to have a lot more joy, a lot more going for her than I did. I stood at my bathroom window and watched her play her guitar for her little girl in her backyard. She played and sang songs of joy, songs of Jesus, songs of praise and all the while she looked so happy I thought she might burst.

I wanted to be like her but I couldn't seem to be that way at all. On the inside I felt friendly toward people but on the outside I had a struggle whenever it came to speaking to someone I didn't know. Years in foster homes had given me a fear of rejection that seemed to get worse as I grew older. Also the years with the Schmidts had handicapped my grammar. Even after four years of college, I knew there were words that I didn't handle correctly. I was comfortable with Russ and our friends and family, but beyond that I had no confidence. As far as joyful went, I knew that I wasn't joyful at all.

Meanwhile, I was learning how to be a mother. I didn't know a baby could be so much work. I had never guessed the love. Many times I was so tired I could hardly keep going. And yet it was worth it.

Then when Dirk was six months old, we received a stunning letter. Dirk's mother had never signed the release for his adoption. The longest days I've ever known followed while we waited for the lawyer to contact her and get her signed release. "What if she changed her mind?" I worried. I thought of my own childhood and what might happen to him if she took him back. What would I do without him? "Dear God, please don't let me lose this baby."

At last the call came—the signing of the necessary papers had gone smoothly.

Our home when Dirk was a baby was an apartment at the back of the school where Russ taught. We had volunteered to be house parents to the school's five teen-aged boarders. To me the boys were no trouble. Extra work was a matter of course and kids without parents always touched a soft part of my heart.

It was about this time that we knew we were ready for another baby. An Indian baby this time we agreed, remembering our early days of marriage on the Indian reservation. Dirk was almost two years old when the phone call came. "We have a baby girl for you," our caseworker announced. I raced down to the gym where Russ was holding basketball practice. Standing beside him on the middle of the court I whispered the good news. "Honey, you're the father of a tiny baby girl." Once more I saw his eyes mist. He took my hand and with basketballs bouncing around us, he thanked God for our new daughter.

Tami was a darling baby with olive skin and deep black hair. Her quiet disposition was so like her Indian heritage. Once again I praised God for the young mother who had allowed us to be the parents of another baby.

Thirteen months later I received an unexpected phone call. It was our caseworker telling us that a little boy had been born a few days earlier and there was no home for him. My heart went out to that boy and I wanted him there, right that minute, but I had to be practical. What would Russ say to three babies in four years? I told the caseworker that I was sorry, but we couldn't handle it.

At noon I said to Russ, "Honey, you'll be proud of me. I actually turned down a baby today."

"You did? How come?"

"I told them that you, I mean we...that...well, are you interested in another baby?"

"I sure am."

By four o'clock we had a new, part-Indian baby sleeping in the other room. We sat around the dinner table, Russ, Dirk, Tami, our five high-school sons, and me and discussed what to name baby number three. One of our big boys, Leo, who was born of missionary parents in Africa, said, "Let's name him after my country." To honor this young boy we had come to think so much of, we agreed. Our newest little son was named Chad.

A year passed. Dirk was four; Tami, two; and Chad, one. Once more it was time for a new baby. Four months later the agency called. A little, part Aleut (Alaskan Indian) girl, Tracy, was welcomed into our family by her brothers and sister. Once again I thanked God that another young mother had allowed her baby to be born.

Shortly after Tracy came, we and our little group of four, moved away from the school into a house. One evening after the children were settled, I sat down beside Russ on our old gray davenport and looked around the room with its hand-me-down furniture. My mind slipped over the past and in an instant I saw a dozen other front rooms, almost all of them as simple as this one. I easily understood that wealth had nothing to do with frayed rugs or scratched tables. Russ was serving the Lord and we were rich in children and in each other. "If only," I thought, "if only I could find that something more that I'm certain the Lord has for us "

Chapter

11

"What are you doing, Mama?" Dirk was always full of questions. I had to admit it was unusual for me to be out in the backyard digging with a serving spoon.

"Honey, I'm digging a hole."

"Why?"

"I'm going to bury something."

"Why?"

"It's a secret. When you get older, I'll tell you all about it. Now you go get your wagon and take Tami for a ride."

He went off to play and I reached in my pocket for the package of cigarettes I'd bought a couple of days before. I knew I had to quit, that my smoking had gone on long enough. I heard someone on the radio tell how they had buried their cigarettes in the ground and had made a little cross over them and that was the end of their smoking. I dropped the remaining cigarettes in the hole and quickly covered them with fresh dirt. Feeling a little foolish, but determined, I placed a cross on the ground. I walked back in the house, craving a cigarette, but knowing at last I was free of smoking.

Terry Watkins was a coach at the school where Russ

taught. He and his wife Connie were two of the nicest people we'd met. That was what made it hard for me to understand why they went to St. Luke's Episcopal Church.

The reason I looked down on St. Luke's was that I'd heard something about a Holy Spirit movement that had begun there. People were being filled with the Holy Spirit and changed, I'd heard. It sounded so much like what I was looking for that I went to see for myself, but it had been a disappointing experience. I'd gone forward to receive the filling of the Holy Spirit but nothing had seemed to happen. Someone had told me I would pray in tongues, but I hadn't believed it when I did. I was told that I would feel joy rising within me but I didn't. The whole experience left me with an uncomfortable feeling, almost an angry feeling towards St. Luke's and particularly people who went there.

Yet Terry and Connie were the friends we enjoyed most. There was something so joyful about them that being with them always made me feel good. Was it their experience at St. Luke's? It couldn't be...or could it?

While I was pondering this, another friend, Joyce Lashua, asked me if I wanted to come to a friend's house and hear Rita Bennett speak. Rita was the wife of Father Bennett who was the pastor at St. Luke's Church. Feeling as I did, I'm not sure why I agreed to come. However, Russ was out of town so I wouldn't have to explain to him what I was doing, and it just seemed like something to do to pass the time. I mumbled something about a meeting to a friend who watched the children. To everyone else I kept completely quiet about it. I didn't want anyone to know that I was going to hear a woman who claimed she had spoken in tongues.

I sat down on the davenport with women on both sides of me and watched others file in until there wasn't a seat left. The conversation rolling around me was almost unreal. One woman said, "I asked Jesus to heal the baby's cough, and now it's gone." Another said, "Jesus worked a miracle for my mother-in-law." Still others said, "Jesus told me I could trust Him to take care of my husband." It seemed that each one had something to say about what Jesus had done or said. They didn't say "Christ" or "Lord" like the people at our church did. They called Him "Jesus" without being embarrassed.

I knew I was in the presence of women who truly knew Him. They knew Him as I longed to know Him. Despite my reservations, I was thrilled. Rita Bennett spoke and I listened carefully as she talked about salvation. I thought, yes, I'm saved and I've asked forgiveness for my sins.

"But there was even more than that," Rita said and she went on and told how she had received the Baptism in the Holy Spirit. She also related how the apostles had been gathered in the upper room and how on the day of Pentecost the Holy Spirit had come upon them and they began to speak in tongues. "They were filled with power and boldness," she said. "Peter, who had previously been such a coward, when questioned about his friendship with Jesus, now had a new power in his life." She continued, "This filling of the Holy Spirit is what gives us power in our Christian lives today. It's that something more we need to be truly alive..."

I listened to every single word. How many times had I honestly cried out for something more? Even back in Alaska when Russ and I just didn't know what we needed, I was certain there had to be more to life than what we had. Lately, I'd known something was missing spiritually from our lives. Could it be the Holy Spirit?

Could it possibly be the Holy Spirit that made Terry and Connie so different from the others I knew? I began to wonder. Had I made a mistake in my judgment of St. Luke's and the baptism in the Holy Spirit? I went home, determined to find out for myself if what Rita Bennett had said was true. I gave the children a hasty dinner and tucked them all in bed much earlier than usual. I just couldn't wait another minute to find out what more the Bible had to say.

When the house was quiet, I sat down in the kitchen and began to read scripture after scripture, checking concordances and cross references and writing as I went. By bedtime I had to conclude that what Rita Bennett said was true.

I called Joyce Lashua and told her I wanted to receive the Baptism of the Holy Spirit. I didn't know what she would say or do, but I hardly expected her to pray over the phone. That's just what she did. She prayed with me that Jesus would baptize me in the Holy Spirit. She told me how to begin speaking in tongues and she even sang me a little song about the love of Jesus. I hung up the phone and felt touched by our Lord God all the way down to my toes.

I knelt by the bed and deliberately began to make a few non-English sounds with my tongue as Joyce had instructed. Then I asked the Holy Spirit to give me a new language. I stayed on my knees, struggling for a long time. Then at last I heard myself say,"A ka lameeda." I decided to write it down. Had I actually spoken in tongues? I went to bed not quite sure.

At three in the morning Tracy woke up for her bottle. I sat in the big chair with her and attempted to speak in tongues again. Once more I said another word and once more I wrote it down. In the morning I gathered up the children and went to see Connie Watkins. I wanted to show her the words I had written down to see if she thought I had spoken in tongues.

"Uh, Connie, uh..." We were sitting in her cheery yellow kitchen. As she poured coffee I struggled to get my words out. I was not good at talking about religious things, anyway, and this whole business of speaking in tongues was embarrassing. I tried it again, "Connie, uh, I wondered if..." I took the little piece of paper I'd written on out of my pocket.

Before I could show it to her, however, Connie put the coffee pot down and came to the table. Looking at me tenderly, she said the most startling thing I'd ever heard, "Fran, the Lord has revealed to me that you are baptized in the Holy Spirit and that you speak in tongues."

I was too surprised to speak and suddenly horrified. If the Lord had revealed that to her, what else did she know? Had He told her about my past? As soon as I could think of a reason to leave, I gathered up the children and sped home.

Again, I tried praying in tongues and once more I could only get a few words. I had to know if I could pray in tongues or not. I went to Joyce Lashua's house to the prayer meeting and quietly explained to her in private why I was there. Nonchalantly, she announced it to everyone else. "Let's pray for a release of Fran's prayer language. Fran would like to speak more fully in tongues."

I felt like I might die of embarrassment. I found myself sitting in a chair in the middle of the room, scared to death, while women laid hands on me and prayed. I was so humiliated the perspiration rolled off my face. "Lord, please give Fran the release of her prayer language and thank you for baptizing her in the Holy Spirit. Praise you, Lord. Thank you, Lord." The women, their hands lightly touching my shoulders and head, kept on praying. "Don't they get tired?" I thought. My own prayers didn't last more than a few minutes. When they began praying in tongues, I heard my own voice say some words that were completely foreign.

"Keep it up, Fran. Praise the Lord."

And I was speaking in tongues. The embarrassment was gone. In its place was a newness, a clean feeling, yes, even joy.

I grew to love the women in that prayer group and would do almost anything to be with them. My friend, Sue, who took care of the children so I could go each week, was amazed at the change in me. Sue and I had both known that the other was a Christian, but we'd never talked about it. Now here I was, talking about the Lord all the time. I was amazed myself; I was even saying the name, "Jesus," without stumbling over it.

Russ didn't know what to make of it. "It's fine for you,

Fran. If you're happy, then so am I." I was spending more and more time in prayer, often praying in tongues for Russ to experience the fullness of the Holy Spirit himself.

The women at Joyce Lashua's prayer group had become my friends. There was a closeness among us that I had never known before in my life, a family feeling, a sharing and a caring to our relationship. In that kind of comfortable setting, I explained how there'd always been a slight chance that I could become pregnant.

"Fran," someone suggested, "let's pray for you to conceive." As they prayed, I fervently prayed for myself.

Eagerly, I waited for the day my period would start. On the scheduled day it didn't come. I knew, I knew a miracle had happened. The following day with still no sign of it, I went out to the doctor's for a pregnancy test. I was halfway there when I felt the undeniably warm trickle that told me my period had begun. I turned the car around and through my tears headed for home.

I paused at the corner store just long enough to buy two packs of cigarettes. As soon as I got the kids down for their naps, I went out in the backyard with an ashtray, both packs of cigarettes and some matches. I sat on the grass and let the anger flow, anger at God, anger that He wouldn't let me get pregnant, anger that I had trused Him to answer my prayer and He hadn't done it.

I lit a cigarette and inhaled deeply. I enjoyed smoking and thought, "If that's the way God is going to be, I will smoke whether He wants me to or not." I lit another one and enjoyed it just as much. In the midst of my anger and rebellion, I heard the Lord speak to me. His words were something I could never have made up. Distinctly I heard, "Enjoy your cigarettes." I reached for another and another and did enjoy them.

Then, there in the midst of that rebellious afternoon, I knew God's presence in a special way. Without words, I was somehow made aware of His voice. He explained that my problem was not smoking, but my rebellion. I understood that He wanted to heal me of the rebellion that made me run for cigarettes whenever I didn't get my own way. He made me realize that I was to quit worrying about smoking and that He would take care of it. No firm resolutions, no burying cigarettes with a cross. I was just to turn it over to Him.

He enveloped me in His goodness and made me understand that it was all right if I wasn't pregnant, all right for Him to be in charge of my life. I sat there on the grass until the children wakened from their naps, just soaking in His goodness, knowing and feeling the special acceptance and love that God Himself had for me and would have all the days of my life.

As the weeks went by, I spent hours pouring over my Bible, reading books and listening to tapes. The subject of the greatest concern to me was the gifts of the Spirit. I wanted to know all there was to know about tongues, interpretation of tongues, prophecy and the word of knowledge. As I studied, I learned something of special interest to me. God gives all His gifts to us so we can lift up, build up and cheer up, but He never uses them to tell us to shape up. As I studied, I realized God would never have revealed anything harmful about my past to Connie Watkins or to anyone. The gifts were to be used now as they had been in the early church to encourage one another, but never to tear anyone down.

I went to the home of a college chum, Jane Hansen, and heard a woman named Shade O'Driscoll teach on the Spirit-filled life. I thought how marvelous it was that Shade, who was just an ordinary housewife like myself, could be teaching on a closer walk with the Lord. Then, to my surprise, when her six-week course was over, someone asked me to teach a series on the gifts. Me! It was incredible! Fran, who a short while ago was so embarrassed to be prayed with that she dripped with perspiration, was being asked to teach. Then I remembered. It was God who was incredible. He can do anything.

The children were becoming bigger and more and more of a joy. One night Russ smiled at me across the table. "Isn't it time for another baby?" he asked.

A few months later the six of us went to the adoption agency to bring home our newest little baby. Tracy, who was three, brought along her dolly; Chad, four, carried a teddy bear; Tami, five, held her doll; and Dirk at seven was my big helper and carried the baby seat. As we got into the caseworker's office, she placed the little blue bundle in Russ' arms. Rusty, named for his new Daddy, was a mixture of Indian, Korean, black and white -- all in five pounds of baby. The children each begged to be the first to hold him. For a moment I stood back and viewed the scene. Russ with the new baby in his arms and the others laughing and chattering. Once more I thanked God for those young mothers who had generously carried on with their pregnancies so that these children of theirs and ours might have life.

Our household with five children under seven was constantly busy, but, nevertheless, Russ and I found time to slip away one Friday evening and attend the information meeting on the baptism of the Holy Spirit at St. Luke's. What a thrilling answer to prayer it was when Russ went up to the altar at the end of the evening and asked to receive the baptism of the Holy Spirit, too.

Chapter 12

The door bell rang. "I'll get it. I'll get it," Chad called. It was his sixth birthday and he'd been waiting on pins and needles all morning for Dottie to arrive. He opened the door and there she stood, a birthday present under her arm, but more importantly THE cake between her hands.

"Auntie, Auntie," Tracy and Rusty called.

"Dottie, come in, let's look at the cake." For each child's birthday Dottie was the one who baked the cake and decorated it with detailed, personalized pictures. In honor of Chad's ancestry, she had piped an Indian boy in colored frosting. Candles made a bonfire in front of his brown-icing teepee. Chad's face beamed as he counted the candles, making sure there were six. I hugged Dottie. "Thank you for being dependable. What would we ever do without you?"

"I love doing it," she replied. Dottie had had a lot of hard bumps in the past few years, including the death of her son, Danny, but she always stayed willing to help others when she was needed. I put my arm around her, gratefully remembering the night she'd gone forward at the Billy Graham meeting. I knew for sure that God was moving in her life, even though at this point only the hardships were visible.

Tami put her hand in Dottie's. "Such a pretty cake, Auntie." Dottie beamed at her niece. Only Dirk looked sad. He stood staring down at the cake as if he were about to cry. "What's the matter?"I asked him.

"It's not fair, " he finally blurted.

"But Auntie made you a cake for your birthday."

"I don't mean the cake. It's just not fair that everybody in this family is Indian, except for me.

Poor Dirk, feeling left out. I slipped over beside him and put my arm around him. Hugging him closely, I reminded him, "Honey, someone has to be the cowboy. Remember, you're the only one from Montana."

With that little bit of wisdom, the crisis passed.

That night, after the birthday celebration was over, I sat beside Chad's bed and we thanked God for the party, the cake and the good day. "Now, let's ask God to bless your mother," I said to the little boy, still wide awake with the day's excitement. Praying for the children's mothers was something we tried to do every so often, but especially on each birthday because, as I explained to the children, their mothers were thinking of them on that day in a special way. Chad closed his little eyes and prayed, "Dear Jesus, please bless my mother today and make her happy." Then he opened his eyes and looked at me. "And thank you for my Mommy and Daddy and Dirk and Tracy and Tami and Rusty and Aunt Dottie, too. Amen."

Meanwhile I was learning that the baptism of the Holy Spirit was only the beginning of what the Lord had waiting for me. One of the joys of my life was the friendship that formed with Shade O'Driscoll, whose husband is one of the pastors at St Luke's. With her, I sometimes shared some hurts of the past that still lingered.

One day Shade said, "Fran, I really can't help you deal with the past, but I know Someone who can." She shared with me how Jesus, who is not limited by time or space, can come into a person's past and heal them.

We got down on our knees one morning in the living room and saw in prayer the little girl of long ago who was lying in bed wanting her Mommy who hadn't been home for a couple of days. "Let Jesus be there with you," Shade said.

I closed my eyes. The loneliness of those days almost seemed to crush me, and then I saw Jesus. He went to the rocking chair and sat down. I saw myself sleeping restlessly, but each time I awoke there He was, silhouetted from the light of the window, caring for me. That healing picture erased the pain of being left alone.

With Shade's help, I went to each of the troubled spots of my life and relived the times of loneliness, of pain, of fear and of terror. In each instance Jesus was there, comforting me until the pain had passed. Through this experience, I found the hurting, rebellious child fading away and a new, secure Fran rising in her place.

Healing of my childhood wounds came to me through many ways. One morning I was sitting at the breakfast nook just plain feeling sorry for myself. All I wanted to do was weep. "God, how can I ever know you as a Father?" I cried out. "I've never known what a father is like."

The Lord said, "What memory do you have of your father?"

"Only one, Lord. He was standing by the high dresser drawer in the bedroom. He reached into his top drawer and pulled out some Hershey bars and a bag of marshmallows and gave them to me."

The Lord said, "That memory is enough to tell you about the kind of Father I am. I give. I am the giver. I gave my Son. I give all that you need."

Little by little, with the help of friends, through prayer, and with God speaking to me I began to understand that I was healed of the wounds of the past. The ugly scars that had marred my inner self were taken away as if the negative effect had never happened. Little by little, Jesus was making me whole.

While all of this was going on in my life, there was in my area of north Seattle something new beginning. Groups of women were getting together once a month to praise God and to tell others about accepting Jesus and the baptism in the Holy Spirit. As these groups began forming all over the country, in Canada and other parts of the world, they became known as Women's Aglow Fellowship International. At Aglow meetings women shared testimonies about what God had done in their lives or they would teach how we are to live as Christian women.

Although women flocked to the meeting, I knew there were other women who had little children who couldn't get out or who lived in remote areas where there weren't Aglows. I began to volunteer my time to Aglow to listen to all the tape recordings of the Aglow meetings and to get the best teaching and the most inspired stories on tape so that women everywhere would not have to be left out.

One day as I was working away with this project, a phone call came from the president of the nearby Aglow. To my surprise, she wanted me to be a speaker at an Aglow meeting. "Me? I don't know. I'll have to pray."

I lost no time getting down on my knees. "Lord, You know I'm not a speaker. You know all the red marks on my papers in college English classes. Lord, You know I'm shy. You know my failures. Teaching a few women in a house is one thing, but speaking to a hundred women . . . Well, Lord . . ."

I did speak to those women, telling them about the little girl without a mother and the miracle God had made of my life. Afterward, a woman came up to me and said, "My life was just like yours. Do you think Jesus could change me, too?" I prayed with her and I sensed God giving me a prophecy for her. He had chosen her for a special ministry in His Kingdom and that He delighted in her.

I remember her joy. "He delights in me? Oh, He knows everything and He still delights?" Tears poured out as she gave her life to Jesus and asked for the baptism in the Holy Spirit.

So the pattern was begun. I would speak and share what God had done for me, and other women would find Him, too. I went through the same self doubt when I was asked to be a retreat speaker. Then God again assured me that all He needed was my willingness and He would make up for my lack. I found that all the studying of scriptures I had done regarding the gifts of tongues, interpretation of tongues, prophecy and the word of knowledge were benefiting me now. Whenever I went I found that I could use the gifts to build up, cheer up and lift up the many, many hurting women whom God loves so much. Then I saw my responsibilities grow until I was the head of the Counseling Ministry and involved in putting Aglow teaching on television.

I wasn't the only one learning, growing and being used by God. At the same time, God was working in Russ. Russ loved teaching and had always remained ready to be a servant. A phone call came asking us to come as a team and speak together. So began husband and wife ministry. Dear God, when I was back in college and took his keys, did you know where all this would lead? It seemed there was no end to what God was going to do.

Little by little I began to understand how all that had happened in my life was being used for good by God. No matter what pain a woman who came to me for prayer had endured, I could relate in some measure and understand. No matter how seamy her life had been, I could tell her mine had been the same but that God had healed me. No matter what she had to say, I wouldn't be shocked or turn away or think her trouble was too much for God. And God used me to tell her He loved her.

Recently at a retreat I was called by the chairman to the First Aid room. Lying on a cot was a woman who had tried to commit suicide, her arms still bleeding from the gashes. I bandaged her arm and firmly told her she was missing the best part of the retreat. Then I took her downstairs where a pastor was just getting ready to give a workshop on coping with condemnation and guilt.

The chairman said later, "You really handled that well, Fran. I just didn't know what to do; you see I've never known anyone who tried to kill themself."

I smiled at her. "Yes, I've had an advantage. You see, I've known someone like that . . ."

Epilogue

On Good Friday, 1978, Linda picked up the telepone and heard a woman's voice ask, "Is this Anna May?" Linda's knees nearly buckled, her heart pounded with the realization of what that question might mean. "Yes," she managed to say, "I'm Anna May."

Anna May had been her name when she'd been a little girl, but somewhere along the way it had been changed. Anyone asking for her by that old name had to be from the long distant past.

For years Linda and I had tried to find our father's family. Mother had told me when I saw her in Chicago that my father had two brothers, Ted and Frank, who had come to Seattle to visit them. I'd written to both names in the Michigan town where she thought they were from, but the letters had produced nothing.

Meanwhile, my father's brother, Ted, who had visited us as a teen-ager, returned to Seattle, determined to find his brother's children. As a last resort, he tried the juvenile authorities. Looking there brought him no help but it did give him an idea.

He returned home and asked his son, a juvenile

worker in Michigan, to look into the problem. His son's official letter brought results: Linda's married name and a Montana location were given. My dad's sister, who works for the phone company in Oregon, began tracking Linda's present phone number from the old one on their records. It was after many tries that she at last heard the words, "Yes, I'm Anna May."

I don't know who was happier, Linda or our aunt. Quickly, the news traveled by phone to one uncle after another. "We found them, we found the children."

On Easter Sunday, the celebration of Resurrection, Linda called me. "Fran, I found Dad's family."

In August a family reunion was planned in Michigan. Fred couldn't get away from his job on the then crucial, Alaska pipeline, but Linda, Dottie and I could hardly wait for the day to come. Seventy-two aunts, uncles, cousins and in-laws from as far as California and Florida, arrived to meet us. They told us that my Dad had twelve brothers and sisters. Some of them hadn't even been born when Dad came West at the age of fifteen. Even more interesting to me, I found that our grandfather was a man of God who'd read the Bible every day and prayed with his children. I felt certain that my grandfather often prayed for us, his grandchildren he never saw. It was even more of a comfort to me to know that my dad had heard the Bible read every day of his life as a boy.

What a time we had, catching up, asking questions, seeing pictures. I walked over the hills that my father had once walked and looked at the same trees his eyes had once seen. At my grandfather's grave I prayed in gratitude for the family I'd found.

I held no bitterness or regret that it had taken so long for us to get together. To my uncles and aunts who might have felt bad that they didn't try harder to find us, I spoke the scripture that came to pass in my life. "If thy father and mother forsake you, the Lord shall take you up."

God's plan is perfect, His timing far better than ours, His ways not our own. No matter who we are or what we've done, God loves us. We are special to Him and He has a plan for our lives. As soon as we give our life to Him, the sooner He can make it into that something beautiful He planned from our very beginning.

SEVEN WAYS THIS BOOK CAN HELP YOU FIND GOD'S PLAN FOR YOU

1) Before Fran was born God knew what her life would be like and the choices she would make. He knew all the hardship and pain, yet He planned to turn it all to good.

List here the pain and problems of your life.

_____

_____

_____

Do you think God is aware of your suffering? _ _ _ _ _

Read these interesting words from His Word:

> And we know that God causes all things to work together for good to those who love God, to those who are called according to His purpose. (Rom. 8:28)

> In Him we also were made [God's] heritage (portion) and we obtained an inheritance; for we had been foreordained (chosen and appointed beforehand) in accordance with His purpose, Who works out everything in agreement with the counsel and design of His own will. So that we who first hoped in Christ— who first put our confidence in Him—have been destined and appointed] to live for the praise of His glory (Eph. 1:11-12 TAB).

God was with Fran every minute just as He is now with you. He used the pain she suffered to give her compassion for others who still suffer from rejection and inferiority. He gave her a special love for children who have no parents. He gave her a heartfelt concern for the lonely that led her into her present work with Aglow television.

Do you think God can use the pain you now suffer to make something beautiful of your life?

_ _

List 4 specific ways you would like God to turn your pain into beauty.

1. _

2. _

3. _

4. _

Prayer: Lord, I can see now that You might even be able to make beauty out of my pain by (fill in the blanks with your above list.)

_ _

_ _

I commit my life and particularly those areas of pain to you to use in these ways or whatever other ways you choose. Amen.

2) Sometimes we think that Jesus only loves us when we are good. We think that when we fight or cause someone pain or are disobedient He stops loving us.

Let's look at Fran's story and the discovery she made:

> "One night as we sat by the fire, smoking our cigarettes and admiring the stars, clear and large in the huge sky, June told me about Jesus' love. 'He loves you no matter what you've done or what you've said or who you've hurt or what thoughts you think. He simply loves you -- right now just as you are.'
>
> "I thought, He couldn't possibly love me. I'm not one of those nicey-nice girls who goes to church. I swear and smoke and drink. Nobody loves a girl like that.
>
> "'He loves you.' June insisted. She told me verses from the Bible that said He did. In verse after verse she explained His love until finally I agreed that she might be right. The only reason I could begin to believe that Jesus loved me just the way I was, was because June had loved me the same way herself."

Fran was surprised to find out that Jesus loved her just as she was. She hadn't known Him, she hadn't lived for Him. Yet He loved her. Her life was filled with things that she thought made her unlovable, yet His love didn't stop.

Is there anything you've done to make you think Jesus couldn't love you? What is it?

- -

- -

117

Read the following words from the Bible carefully:

> In Him we have redemption through His blood,
> the forgiveness of our trespasses, according to
> the riches of His grace, which He lavished
> upon us (Eph. 1:7-8).

> For God so loved the world, that He gave His
> only begotten son, that whoever believes in
> Him should not perish, but have eternal
> life. For God did not send the Son into the
> world to judge the world, but that the world
> should be saved through Him (John 3:16-17).

What do these words tell you about Jesus' love for you?

_ _

Jesus puts no conditions on His love. He loves you today
just exactly as you are. His love is consistent; it will
never go away or change.

Prayer: Dear Jesus, I have decided to accept Your love for
me even though I don't feel it, and I realize that You love
me exactly as I am. I confess that I thought you could not

love me because I have _ _ _ _ _ _ _ _ _ _ _ _ _ _ _ _ ,
but I now realize that this isn't true. Your love will never
go away or change. Thank you. Amen.

Now read Psalm 103:12:

> As far as the east is from the west, so far has He
> removed our transgressions [sins] from us.

3) Even though God loves you unconditionally and can make something beautiful from your life, He needs your cooperation to make it happen.

The following scripture will mean a lot to you:

> Behold, I stand at the door and knock; if anyone hears My voice and opens the door, I will come in to him, and will dine with him, and he with Me (Rev. 3:20).

It tells you Jesus wants to come into your life in a special way. He's knocking at the door of your heart. Will you open that door and ask Him to come in?

_ _

If you answered, "Yes," to the last question, write the date here. _
It is your own special "commitment card."

The next step is to let Him forgive you your sins.

Read the following words from the Bible:

> . . . and the blood of Jesus His Son cleanses us from all sin (I John 1:7 NASB).
> He is faithful and righteous to forgive us our sins and to cleanse us from all unrighteousness (I John 1:9 NASB).

What makes God able to forgive your sins?

(Fill in the blanks) The _ _ _ _ _ _ _ _ _ _ of Jesus

on the cross _ _ _ _ _ _ _ _ _ _ away my sins.

Now read Fran's conversation with Dottie:

"I answered her as best I could, 'Yes, when Jesus died, He took away all the punishment for my sins. When I asked Him to forgive me, He did. Every sin I've ever committed in my whole life has been forgiven and my life has started all over.'

"Dottie looked with hope. 'I wish my sins were forgiven.'

"'They can be, Dottie if you'll ask.'"

Come to Jesus right now. Confess every sin, no matter how little or how big. Ask Him to forgive you.

Prayer: Lord, I understand that you want to forgive ALL my sins. Please forgive me for _ _ _ _ _ _ _ _ _ _ _ _

_ _

I choose to believe that You have already forgiven me and forgotten all my sins. I am free to be the kind of person You want. Thank you.

The following Scripture will make you feel great:

"Come now, and let us reason together," says the Lord. "Though your sins are as scarlet, they will be as white as snow: though they are red like crimson, they will be like wool" (Isa. 1:18).

Let the wicked forsake his way, and the unrighteous man his thoughts; and let him return to the Lord, and He will have compassion on him; and to our God, for He will abundantly pardon (Isa. 55:7).

Isn't that good news? Not only are those confessed sins forgiven, they are blotted out, made clean, FORGOTTEN by God.

4) Becoming a Christian and confessing your sins is the big step that allows God's great plan for you to begin in your life. It would be wonderful if none of us ever sinned again after we became Christians. However, the fact of the matter is: we do sin, all of us sin, over and over, more often than we would ever want to admit. Yet every time we sin, God is willing and ready to forgive us.

Listen to the following scripture:

> For Thou, Lord, art good, and ready to forgive, and abundant in loving-kindness to all who call upon Thee (Ps. 86:5 KJV).

> And behold, there was a woman in the city who was a sinner; and when she learned that He was reclining at the table in the Pharisee's house, she brought an alabaster vial of perfume, and standing behind Him at His feet, weeping, she began to wet His feet with her tears, and anointing them with the perfume. Now when the Pharisee who had invited Him saw this, he said to himself, "If this man were a prophet He would know who and what sort of person this woman is who is touching Him, that she is a sinner" (Luke 7:37-39).

> But Jesus was saying, "Father forgive them; for they do not know what they are doing" (Luke 23:34).

Let's read about the way Fran handled the sin in her life after she became a Christian:

> "All day long I went over the guilt of that experience, telling myself how I'd failed. By evening time it occurred to me what to do, something I should have done immediately. Down on my knees in my room, I prayed, 'Jesus, please forgive me again. I'm sorry. I want in my heart to turn from this kind of sin forever.' In that moment of seeking forgiveness, the weight of the guilt slipped from my shoulders. How could I accuse myself when the Lord Jesus had already forgiven me?"

Since she confessed her sin and asked God's forgiveness what two things happened?

1 _

2 _

In Fran's words:

> "Although I later wrote Philip a letter asking his forgiveness, the whole episode never brought any guilt again, and soon became nothing more than another forgiven shadow of the past."

List the sins you still feel guilty about

1. _

2. _

3. _

4. _

Prayer: Heavenly Father, I have been feeling guilty about

_ _

_ _

I realize now that You don't want me to feel guilty and since I have just confessed my sins to You and You have forgiven me, I don't have to feel guilty about them ever again. Amen.

5) There's something wonderful and special about friendships. Our friends weave the fabric of our lives and that fabric would be dull without them. None of us wants to be without at least one friend. Yet our choice of friends is important in allowing God's plan to work in our lives. Let's look at Fran's dilemma:

> "'Who are you going to hang around with this year?' I asked her.
> "'I'm not sure. What about you?'
> "'I don't know either. I know I'd fit in with the wild kids. I'm just not sure about the others, but they seem okay.' I went back and forth in my mind. Both groups were appealing. One, because I was so familiar with it; the other, because I felt an almost unexplainable pull towards it.
> "Finally one morning as we kicked our way through crisp mounds of brown autumn leaves, I told Dottie I'd made my decision. I'm not going to get mixed up with the wild kids. I think I'm supposed to stay away from people that would get me in trouble."'

Maybe we don't have to pick between two groups, one wrong for us and one right, but most of us know someone who is the wrong friend for us to have right now. When we're with that person we do things we wouldn't do if he or she weren't around.

Think over your life. Is there someone who is the wrong

friend for you? _

Read this word from God:

> Do not enter the path of the wicked, and do not proceed in the way of evil men. Avoid it, do not pass by it; turn away from it and pass on. For they cannot sleep unless they do evil (Prov. 4:14-16).

> My son, if sinners entice you, do not consent . . . My son, do not walk in the way with them. Keep your feet from their path (Prov. 1:10,15).

Do you think life will be lonely without that person to talk to or walk with or call on the phone? Talk it over with your friend, Jesus. Tell Him how you feel. *He understands.* Ask Him to give you the right friends for you. Wait for that friend. You'll be thrilled!

Write down the names of some people you know who would be the RIGHT friends.

_ _

_ _

Choose one person that you would like to get together with this week. Make specific plans.
Write down what you did. How did God bless your time together?

_ _

_ _

_ _

Don't forget that God loves the friend(s) that you know is not good for you right now. Even though you won't be seeing them as often, be sure to pray for them every day.

Prayer: Lord, I really want to please you. I've thought it over carefully and realize that _ _ _ _ _ _ _ _ _ _ _ _

_ _ _ _ _ _ _ _ _ _ _ _ _ _ _ _ is not a good influence on my life right now. I may be lonely without (him/her), but I know that You will fill that gap in my life with other friends who will help me. I also know that You love

_ _ _ _ _ _ _ _ _ _ _ _ _ _ _ _ and would like to give (him/her) the kind of friends that will be good for (him/her). Amen.

6) Even with good friends there comes a time when we find ourselves hurt by them. Or perhaps like Fran you have been hurt by a parent or relative; perhaps you were abandoned or discarded or misunderstood by someone you love and who should love you.

Forgiving everyone who hurts you, or who has ever hurt you, will assist you even more in becoming the person

God has planned for you to be. Not only that -- His Word asks you to forgive.

Thoughtfully read what He has to say:

> "And if he sins against you seven times a day, and returns to you seven times, saying, 'I repent,' forgive him" (Luke 17:4).

> And be kind to one another, tender-hearted, forgiving each other, just as God in Christ also has forgiven you (Eph. 4:32).

> Bearing with one another and forgiving each other, whoever has a complaint against anyone; just as the Lord forgave you, so also should you (Col. 3:13).

Choose one verse to write in your own words.

\- \-

\- \-

Now read again Fran's words of forgiveness:

> "I forgive her, Jesus. I forgive her for leaving us when we were little, for not coming to see us, for not writing. I forgive her for being an alcoholic and for the way she lives. I forgive her, Jesus. I forgive her. I forgive her for not asking about my life, for not asking about the others. I forgive her for getting drunk..." Slowly, as I forgave, the Lord showed me something I hadn't understood before. Mother couldn't come and see us because she couldn't handle the guilt. She

couldn't ask about the last 15 years because the guilt of her leaving us was too great, and the guilt that kept her from asking about the others was the guilt that was keeping her an alcoholic.

"Jesus, I do forgive her. I hold nothing against her. Please bless her. Heal her and bring her to know You as her Savior."

Now think of the person who has hurt you most. Will you forgive that person as Fran forgave her mother?

- -

How about the others who have hurt you? Will you forgive each of them?

- -

It may take days, even weeks to forgive all the people who have hurt you. Jesus will bring them to your mind one by one so that you can forgive them . . . and get on with His plan for your life.

Make a list of the people you need to forgive. After each name write down the date that you forgive (him/her).

- -

- -

- -

Read what the Bible has to say about forgiveness:
And whenever you stand praying, forgive, if you have anything against anyone; so that your Father also who is in heaven may forgive you your transgressions (Mark 11:25).

Rewrite this verse in your own words, using specific names of people as they fit.

_____

_____

_____

Prayer: Friend Jesus, as I look back over my life I see that I have been hurt by many people and that I have allowed those hurts to pile up in my life. Right now I ask Your help in forgiving _____

_____

Please bring to my mind each person I am holding things against so that I can forgive (him/her), thus clearing my life to receive your complete forgiveness. Amen.

7) We sin; we are forgiven. Our lives get on with God's plan for us. That's good news!

It's time to raise our goals even higher. Some call it resisting temptation. It could be called passing a test. There will come a time when we are tempted to sin and yet will want to do God's will so much we'll say no to that temptation.

Read again Fran's temptation:

"A thousand emotions it seemed went through me. I was in love with this man. I felt in my own body that I wanted his love. He was the strong one. If he said it was okay, then it probably was. Yet, I knew, deep down, I knew, that engaged or not, in love or not, that this was sin. God had given us rules for our own good. He meant for us to keep them. Somehow I also knew that this was a test. It didn't matter that Russ was young and virile. It was that very fact that made the test so real. And it was a test that God allowed."

And her answer:

"'No, Russ, we have to wait.'

The moment was over. The test was passed."

Fran understood that God would have forgiven her but what she didn't fully understand until later is that by saying no to temptation she gained a special gift from God.

"Some time went by before I understood a little of what the test had been about. If we'd sinned, God would have forgiven us and we would have started all over again, that was true. But would Russ ever have totally trusted me?

On the other hand, passing the test brought a blessing that overwhelmed me as I considered it in the days ahead. My confession of the past had deeply alarmed Russ. Now he would always know that the past was over, that I could be trusted and that he would never have to doubt me."

God gave Fran a gift. A married life built on trust, a married life free from degrading suspicion, a special gift from God for saying no to temptation, for passing a difficult test.

In your life you'll be tested, too. If you flunk the test you'll be forgiven. If you pass you can go on to greater and greater things, discovering even more of God's great plan for you.

If you have been a Christian for a while, you can probably think of some "tests" you have taken. Write down the ones which were most important and whether you passed or not. Also write the results of "passing" or "failing."

_ _

_ _

_ _

Whether you have been a Christian for a long time, or have just given your life to Jesus, the next time you face a temptation, write down what it is and what you should do about it.

_ _

_ _

_ _

Prayer: Dear Lord, please help me to make the right choices when I face temptation. I accept Your forgiveness for the times I "flunked" your "tests" in the past. Thank you for loving me whether I "pass" or "fail." In everything, help me to learn more about Your will for my life.

Think about this:

> "... forgetting what lies behind and reaching forward to what lies ahead, I press on toward the goal for the prize of the upward call of God in Christ Jesus" (Phil. 3:13b, 14).

TO SUMMARIZE

Answer yes or no:

1. I have committed my pain to God.

- -

2. I know that no matter what I have done, Jesus loves me.

- -

3. I know that my sins are forgiven.

- -

4. I no longer feel guilty about any specific sins.

- -

5. I am letting God direct my friendships.

- -

6. I have forgiven (or am in the process of forgiving) everyone who has hurt me in the past.

- -

7. When I am tempted, I am learning to ask for God's help in making the right decisions.

- -

If you answered no to any of the questions above, you might want to go back through the study from that number on. It is also a good idea to review these questions from time to time, to be sure that you can still answer yes to each one. There may be areas of your life which will need a spiritual up-date from time to time.